GROWING YOUR OWN MONEY

First Published in 2019 by Dean Thorpe.
Thorpe House, 9 School Lane, Dronfield S18 1RY

ISBN 978-1-5272-3886-2

Printed by Amadeus Press,
Ezra House, West 26 Business Park, Cleckheaton, West Yorkshire BD19 4TQ.
Tel: (01274) 863210. E-mail: info@amadeuspress.co.uk.
Website: www.amadeuspress.co.uk

Contents

Foreword

When asked to write a foreword for this book and then to discover it was about Money, I wondered if I was the right person to do this. And then I realised that we are all experienced at using money and I didn't have to be an expert on the subject. I have read a few books on the subject and there are many more titles that we could explore.

Naturally I understand why Dean Thorpe is qualified to share ideas about it, because he is in the money business, and what I like is the fact that this isn't just for financial advisers per se, or investors or entrepreneurs looking for their 'ticket' to greater success.

This book is written for the broadest possible audience - everyone, and one of my overriding thoughts as a training and educational professional was that this book could be great as part of a school curriculum or to be included in apprentice training programmes by employers. Why is it that we all left school without any understanding of money?

I understand there have been a few changes where some basic money training is given these days at school and these lessons are practical about housekeeping and staying out of debt which is all good stuff. How about ideas on using money to create a better life? Attaining a better attitude around money, and how to discard and remove beliefs that could be standing in the way of making money work for you rather than the other way around.

I first met Dean Thorpe when he was a young man many years ago. He got my attention early on as someone who enjoyed meeting people and was open minded and very positive in his attitude to business, new ideas and life itself.

Knowing him as I do, he's the sort of person you could invite into a meeting on an important or even routine issue. By inviting him to lead it, he would get more contributions, interaction from people present, and create an enjoyable process that leads to significant decision making, tangible outcomes and next steps.

If he takes the same approach here, which I know he will, then we are in for some extraordinary insights which will be worth both the financial investment to buy this book and the time investment to read it.

I'm very keen to see what Dean has in store for us in this book, especially as I'm wondering if there are any tools, tips and techniques that he hasn't yet shared with me (and should have done!).

Thank you, Dean, in advance and I wish you every success with this new book.

David Butterfield
Head of Learning and Development, Aggregate Industries
December 2018

Preface

Take a look at this book. No, I mean really take a look at it as a tangible item in your hands. Carefully observe its size, print, layout, font and jacket. How does it feel in your hands? Are you looking forward to reading it? (I hope so!) Because in presenting new ideas to you, for me it's not just a record of words on a page. I am trying to create a complete experience. If you are going abroad on holiday, you would normally see the flight as part of the overall experience. So I have fashioned this book with the same thing in mind, yet everything here is designed to have a deeper message. More money in your life will give you a better experience of life, and the means to achieve this is about offering a better experience to other people in ways that they are pleased to pay you for.

This final outcome, my book to you called *Growing Your Own Money* came from thoughts I had long before I wrote a single word. I decided what I needed to do at a single point in time when it felt intuitive and right despite my mental chatter thinking about alternative titles around my passion for self-development.

This book wasn't a passing thought, or one on a list of possibilities; it is an idea that had come into its time rather than a feeling of keeping up with colleagues and friends who had also written books. It was a strong desire to communicate something I genuinely wanted to share with others.

In life, I am extremely grateful for what I have. This includes a wonderful wife, amazing children and a stable and satisfying business. To many I am wealthy in that I'm running my own successful family business, employing a workforce and yes, I definitely have a great relationship with money.

Then I have to, because I advise others how to make their own money last longer and how to grow what they already have to maximum advantage. But this book is not about offering financial advice.

When I think back to my childhood and imagine some of the thoughts I had, indeed we all have, about growing up and who and what we might become. A very chilling question we should all reflect upon and ask ourselves now is: "How proud would the child I was… be of the person I have become?" One of the primary reasons for the answer to be in the negative is very often to do with lack of money, money mis-management or an ignorance of how to 'grow' more of it.

In thinking long and hard about this book, it soon became clear to me that there are plenty of money books out there that I would largely place into three categories:

1. The "How to" series… 'How to become Super Rich', 'How to Invest and become Wealthy', 'How to set up a Business and make "loads" of Money', 'How to make money while you sleep and do no work whatsoever.' You get the idea.

2. The 'Spiritual' category which is about universal laws, and in most recent times "the Law of Attraction'. This is essentially about holding the thought in your head of how much or what you most want and the desired result will eventually materialise. Many scoff but actually aren't we rather good at the opposite? Thinking of something negative and guess what - it happens!

3. The 'Business Related' subjects which is very much MBA material made simple, suggesting that the best way to make money is to run your own business in an orthodox way, but with a twist here and there.

Ignoring the first category, categories two and three do have some merit and I will certainly be happy to share the best parts of what I perceive these ideas to be. Yet there is a fourth category that I rarely find in a book on money which made me want to write this one.

It is a category that's worthy of some significant thought because my fervent belief is that the majority of people who feel they have a lack of money can change their fortunes in some very simple ways that perhaps they have never considered. When these ideas or applications come together they create an open door, which can and does change lives, sometimes in extraordinary ways.

My own success with money came from joining the family business and in recent years contributing in a way that has grown the business and increased my personal wealth and well-being substantially.

Two things I would like to share upfront is the fact that one of the factors that has made the biggest difference is being aware very early on that my mindset and attitude could have a huge impact on future goals, dreams, ambitions and success. Thankfully, in my early development my father, who I will be eternally grateful to, introduced me to this way of thinking and the results that emerged started my road to a better life in an extremely positive way.

The second thing was that I never ever set out to find a career specifically to make lots of money. This was never in my head at the start, and though I wanted to do well in my life my focus was on what to do well rather than how much it would pay me. And is this not true with the majority of people on this planet?

Most people have chosen an occupation for what it's about… how much they enjoy doing it… and whether it would make them genuinely happy. I also appreciate that many people don't have that choice and sometimes have to just take what's given. These people actually do have a choice. They can start looking for what they really want to do with their lives or they can carry on with the job they have.

THE BIRTHDAY PRESENT

Not long ago my wife gave me an unusual present. As someone who obviously knows me very well, she bought me a flying lesson. Within 30 minutes of being in the air I had already decided to learn to fly which I then subsequently did, and isn't it curious how life seems to support those who want to help themselves. To many this concept is hearsay, for me it happens all the time.

So it was no surprise after getting my pilots license that I had an opportunity to buy a share in an aircraft. This has all happened in an extremely short space of time and admittedly I was able to afford this project where many people may not have the money to do so. Yes I look back on my life and I can pick out the same thing happening in other ways. On this occasion this has been presented to me, which has led to a need to take action and build on this opportunity. The reason I am sharing this with you is because I like to think that I am about to present something to you which is an opportunity for you to improve the quality of your life immeasurably for the better, and all I ask is you have an open mind, read the contents of this book at least once and ideally a couple of times; make plenty of notes and think about the various concepts and finally be prepared to put the ideas into action.

Naturally, I am not asking you to put all the ideas into action, however you will know intuitively the things you absolutely should do, many of which you may have started before and not completed on, or that you used to do before and for some reason you stopped. By the way, there is a very strange human trait, which you may or may not be aware of that's worth mentioning right now. Quite simply it's that when we take up a new activity, make it a habit and notice that it works, we often then stop doing it! It happens around diets, personal habits and money related matters all the time. Why did we start a savings account, save for 18 months regularly, and then decide to spend the money and never save again? Why do we start that fabulous exercise regime that made us feel better and look better and then we stopped it when we realised it was actually working. It makes no sense, or does it?

I would say that we as a species are master saboteurs of our own lives. We do not want to be yet we often are at a subconscious level. For many it's not fear of failure it's actually a fear of success and this fear is embedded in our hearts and minds from things that have probably happened to us, or simply said to us in childhood.

This is why parents can have a massive impact on their children because what they might portray around money matters can make that child happy and content with sufficient money in their future or consistently poor in relative terms always scratching around to make ends meet. If you have children who are very young, you can give them an extraordinary gift that will help them throughout their lives. That gift is the right attitude and beliefs around what money truly is.

If I were to now go on to confirm that money and tangibles should be something that we must all spend more time acquiring for its own sake then this book would be purely a 'How to' in category 1. Where I do want to offer some grounded suggestions so this is not all limp theory, I want to confirm now before we go any further that the reason there is so much mental poverty around money in the world is that people put money first, which is always the biggest mistake. If you look at the evidence in the form of biographies of some of the richest people that ever lived, very few put money first. Those that did probably pillaged and stole their wealth because their focus was on tangibles. What this book is about is putting money second or even third where it comes to you as a result of doing other things first.

There will also be an element of changing and re-evaluating some of your deep-rooted beliefs about money and your relationship with it. However, I hope above all else this does end up as a catalyst to bigger and better things where you can upgrade your life and happiness and notice that one of the spin-off consequences is that your financial wealth and well-being has also increased in the process.

The purpose of this preface is to gently ease into this subject and get your mind open in a receptive way in order that my words to you have some immediate value. I can't imagine that every person who reads this book is necessarily going to agree with everything in it, yet if you are able to take away a few ideas at the end and these ideas make a difference to you, then my task has been a worthy one!

Also in this preface, I want to share the fact that I thought about offering an alternative word for the concept of money. In the end I realised that this would not work because any word I came up with would be based on my own personal understanding of what money is, rather than allow you the reader to work this out for yourself. So when I use the word money, I do mean what most people see as currency, funds, collateral and financial wealth in a number. What this book is about is re-defining our appreciation and understanding of the significance of 'money' and what it could really mean. The fact that this word is potentially hiding the truth of living a more fulfilled and contented life by focusing on this not the money most of us assume must come first.

Here are two lists. If you could choose one, which one would you go for? Bear in mind you would get EXACTLY what's on the list. Nothing more, nothing less.

List A

- expensive cars (2)
- two magnificent homes in locations of your choice
- clothes and personal possessions
- 4 fabulous holidays a year
- lots of money to spend on your favourite hobby
- private education and health for the family
- money to host functions for friends regularly
- a generous monthly spending allowance and lots of money in the bank

List B

- Happiness & contentment for the rest of your life
- A family home of your own and basic transport
- Lots of time to do what you want
- The freedom to decide what you did each day
- Support to be healthy and fit
- The choice to be able to focus on life, not surviving in it
- Peace of mind in all aspects of life

If you notice, List A does tend to draw you in. There's a glitz about it that immediately attracts most people where List B sounds good, but lacks the glitz and you may even be looking at it wondering if these items would make you happy. Of course there's nothing to say you can't have both, but unless you already have one of these lists, it would be unusual for you to have picked up this book and read so far… therefore I have to assume that you have neither in the quantity that you desire and so we're back to making you choose. If you had to choose one, which one would it be?

I am hoping you do choose B, because though I can help with A, you need to have the 'B Mindset' in order to attain B first which can then more easily allow A. I hope this makes sense. And if it doesn't yet, it certainly will by the end of the book. The book is split into three broad areas.

Part 1: MONEY-HEART

'Heart' is about deep understanding, intuition, gut feeling and what is true for you and potentially what is true about money. It's the starting place where we look at some broad concepts and ideas - in particular ten money concepts.

Part 2: MONEY-HEAD

'Head' is more down to earth, considered, accepted and where the world sees money both as an incentive and tool. Here I am hoping you will glean little 'gems' or 'nuggets' that you can take away, polish and use yourself.

Part 3: MONEY-HANDS

This is the hands-on element which is an all-important aspect. It relates to responding to the ideas in the book and taking action. This will be my own 'How to' version of thoughts though it will not relate to quick fixes, doing something for nothing, getting rich overnight or being motivated by endless riches where happiness doesn't seem to figure anywhere.

This *Heart-Head-Hands concept* is nothing new. Many would see it as a kind of Mind,

Body and Soul approach. However, the latter sounded a bit more 'out there' where the former is I hope more down to earth and easier to understand.

There's also something called a *False Dilemma*. This is when you have a challenge and a decision to be made where you automatically go into 'this solution or that solution' mode. In other words two options. It's false because there are often a myriad of options for every dilemma — many, many shades of grey rather than it being black and white. The solution or new way forward for you after reading *Growing Your Own Money* is probably going to be some of this idea, some of that and a few other tools thrown in. This combination may be perfect for you but not for everyone. The main thing is that you get something that's completely MAD. In other words, makes a difference.

Whatever way you want to see it, I am now mentally rolling my sleeves up and wish to tempt you on to the virtual high diving board of your mind as we together push off and plunge deep into the waters of an alternative insight into money. Please join me in climbing now and climb the ladder.

Dean Thorpe
Dronfield, Sheffield, 2018

Part One

MONEY HEART

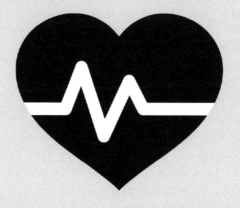

Top Money Concepts, myths that may hold your heart back, mind over money, basic ideas to get your money seeds planted… Growing Your Own Money

1

Growing Your Own Money

"Lazy Hands Make for Poverty, but Diligent Hands bring Wealth"
Proverbs 10-4

Wouldn't it be amazing to be able to buy a packet of money seeds, then place them in the garden, water them daily and have crisp legal bank notes grow like leaves possibly producing up to £500 a day, every day? Of course money seeds in the literal sense are not available the last time I checked, however I would like to think that this book is the nearest you will get to them.

The way I have shaped *Growing Your Own Money* is to blend the two professional sides of my career. The first and main side is as a qualified independent financial adviser with personal and business clients, and my other side as a personal development professional where I have helped individuals and addressed UK and international audiences of subjects relating to becoming more efficient, effective and ultimately more successful.

In this book I want to engage you in both ways. One in a very grounded manner giving you insights into how others, especially successful business people, have attained success as well as the flip side where people have used their creativity, originality, mindset and overall positive attitude to uncover many things they already had available to them - I refer to skills and latent abilities - that they were then able to use to great effect.

I believe that both these aspects are important and that you can't have any realistic chance of dramatically improving your money situation and overall wealth with just one element.

By the way, this does not mean you will have to have a business to be super successful, though understanding more about this side of how the world works and the attached opportunities available, it could mean that you are able to read between the lines and come away with something significant that works for you.

There can only be four reasons why anyone would want to read a book about money, and if you allow me a little wriggle room I'd like to suggest you are in one of these four groups:

1: You like to Study Books about Money

I would be surprised if you are in this first group. I am not sure there are many people who study the subject of money. If however you have bought this book for that sole purpose, I would be delighted if you contact me after reading it at **dean@deanthorpe.com** with some feedback, particularly letting me know what you learned from it. In reality, you're more likely to be in one of the other three groups.

2: You Lack Enough Money

If you fall within this group you're probably in the majority. I have some good news for you and I also have some better news for you. The good news is that this book will definitely put you on the right road to increasing the amount of money in your life. It may not happen overnight - in fact I can guarantee it's not going to happen overnight, but within a relatively short time period of, shall we say, 12 to 18 months, you will be in a better place provided you follow through on the relevant action steps that relate to your situation. The better news, is that the way you make this happen is a lot easier than you may imagine.

3: You Have Money and Want Much More

I predict this would be the second largest group. And here is also something positive for you. This group is likely to make the biggest strides forward to improve their lives in the shortest time frame.

This is because if you already have money, achieving more *in a different way* will be something you can readily switch to. It's like you've been going down the wrong path in a forest, but you're already running, simply needing a different route.

4: You are Money-Comfortable and interested in New Opportunities

If you are in this, probably the smallest group, you may have a sticking point. The Challenge is that you could be stuck in your ways. If you have money and acquired it by a certain methodology that worked for you, for you to now pick up new tips and ideas is fine, however are you likely to revert to type and not actually change anything you're doing? All I would ask is that you step back and think hard about any idea here and seriously consider what might happen if you followed through on it.

Whatever your reason is for reading this book my advice is to read it through once, then a second time making notes or highlighting passages. Then act on what you most feel would be a good way forward using your heart first not your head.

Reverting to Type

This has always been a big eye opener for me. I remember attending a seminar with

600 people. The presenter was an expert in human behaviour (apparently!) and in one of the breaks, a lady irritated him with a question and I watched aghast as the man suddenly reverted to type…his true self! It was quite shocking. After all that he had said on stage and after all the notes I took on his words of wisdom, I now felt cheated, hollow and empty. Needless to say I didn't stay for the rest of the event.

Reverting to who you truly are can be good and bad. If you are a karate expert who never talks about it, but then threatened in the street late at night makes you revert to type and defend yourself and your family, this is a good reversion. The other way around however is a major problem. Saying you are open minded, prepared to be committed to something then reverting to a closed mind, negativity and no commitment means that nothing you ever read or learn will ever make any difference to you whatsoever. And unless you are able to deal with this glitch in your personality, there's little point hoping that by reading this book you are likely to ever benefit, because reading it is one thing; following through and acting on the ideas and advice is wholly required which is why I am stressing the point at length.

Re-Evaluating 'Money' Associative Conditioning

Imagine this. You spend a couple of hundred pounds on something using a plastic card, then make two hundred pounds selling something on Ebay. Let's say these two transactions are both £200. Which one has the greater financial significance? May I suggest it's the latter? Another example is that you may fill up your car with fuel on a forecourt and spend £50. Then you make £50 at an auction where you've been hanging around for a few hours, getting the item ready to sell, and so on. The same question…

The first transaction buying fuel, you don't even think about, the second one making £50 has more resonance, purpose and meaning so you would probably drive home from the auction with a big smile on your face thinking about a successful day. Two totally different outcomes of the same transactional value. Makes no sense? Or does it? There is no question that a lot of us have been programmed to think about money in a certain way and this program, a bit like a piece of computer software is what runs your financial thinking and eventual money outcomes. Garbage in, garbage out, all that you are putting to your mental software will emerge as a stark reality. It might be time to completely re-evaluate money; not only what it is and what it does for you, but also what it will mean to you after you read this book.

It seems an unusual idea of evaluating money for what it was. Does it even matter? I refer to your past relationship with it and how that has shaped and modelled the basis of your mental computer software program.

10 Money Considerations To Begin

Taking a step further, I wonder if any of the following 10 money considerations are already part of your programming? If the ideas are not and you think they have value, perhaps they should be included in the program update. These concepts I have researched over the years in both giving financial advice and in business consulting with SMEs (small to medium size enterprises). They have also been useful at business conferences where I have been a guest speaker. The point is that these ideas may have a personal or business significance or a combination of the two.

Consideration One: Debt is a Disease

If you were brought up to believe you could catch something really unpleasant from going into the red, do you think there would be any debt? I doubt it. People would do what they always used to do in the past and simply go without until they could afford it. Credit cards only came to the UK in 1972, and that started a debt revolution. Before it was not so easy to borrow money, and therefore people generally didn't do it unless it was for a large purchase. It's sad to say but debt is a financial product sold by large institutions who make colossal sums on impulse buying and consumers who lack the full appreciation for the dangers of debt.

Mortgages are bad enough where you pay for your house many times over, and the recent phenomena of pay day lending with the most obnoxious and unbelievable interest rates that are more akin to being 'a scam', continues to shock me as a financial adviser. Yet having a few thousand percent as an interest rate is apparently not a crime. It's a mad world we are living in. I am covering debt right at the beginning, more to get it out of the way, because if you are in debt, even major debt and are just about managing, then you have every chance to turn this disadvantage or 'disease' into a positive. Disease is of course dis-ease and who wouldn't be, with lots of expensive credit hanging around your ears unhelpfully. Even worse, banks offering you even more credit and still calling themselves 'responsible lenders'.

Surely responsibility would be better seen as tempting people to save instead of continually tempting them to use credit - but then there's not so much profit in helping your customer by saving. The way to rid yourself of the disease is to get a proper view of each and every debt. In my experience most people bury their heads in the sand until its too late or very nearly too late to do something sensible about it.

Some things to consider working out if you have some debt sooner rather than later:

- can you take the debt to someone cheaper?
- can you negotiate in order to pay it back faster?
- can you get a zero interest loan and pay it off earlier?
- can you ask family for help at zero/low interest and pay it back to them?
- can you sell anything and raise debt repayment capital?
- can you start saving to pay off debts one by one in chunks?

In my experience of advising clients in debt, I found that those who got the 'disease' out in the open or under the microscope as it were, with the desire to eradicate it before it became terminal, created a slow momentum which built up to a powerful force of successful removal of the unwanted situation with all the relief one gets from taking positive action. Those that took the advice and did nothing probably still suffer from the disease today.

If you are not managing your debts well, you should seek the advice of an insolvency practitioner. One of the best places I can suggest people turn for serious debt advice is **www.CAPuk.org**. You can call them on 0800 328 0006.

If debt has really gotten out of control and you feel it has got to a 'terminal' situation, it may even be time to consider bankruptcy. If that was your decision or a recommended outcome by a debt adviser, rest assured that you'd be in good company (not that I suggest you should consider it for that reason). Abraham Lincoln was not great with money and was made bankrupt on several occasions and in modern times the list includes *Kim Basinger, George Best, Donald Trump, Francis Ford Coppola, Walt Disney, M C Hammer, LaToya Jackson, Meat Loaf, Burt Reynolds, Michael Barrymore, Sarah Ferguson* and many more. It's not the end of the world and could be the start of a much better one. Enough said.

CONSIDERATION TWO:
THE HUMAN IMAGINATION IS A VALUABLE COMMODITY

Take a long hard look around you. Wherever you are currently standing or sitting just about everything you see started out in the mind of a human being save creation itself.

For example, I can see a clock, desk light, telephone, mobile phone, laptop computer, flat screen television, UPVC windows, venetian blinds and so on. Each and every item began as a thought in the human imagination. Certainly, there are people who have invented things and got very little for it, yet the majority have ultimately made a fortune.

Whenever I have a conversation with someone about the power and value of the human imagination they often look back at me as if to say:"Are you suggesting, I come up with an original idea that makes a lot of money?" Of course that would be great, but you couldn't be more astute than that.

Jerry Baldwin, Zev Siegl and Gordon Bowker founded Starbucks in 1971. They had 'invented' a slightly different way to sell coffee. Needless to say their twist on an existing project has been astonishingly successful in a relatively short time space. The fortune that they have made is not based on anything totally original, it's much more about having a clever idea, or even just a creative one.

In this book we will see a few businesses that have been inventive and creative without being totally original. Indeed there is much to suggest that being totally original is a more difficult proposition then a twist on something that already exists. The reason is that the completely original concept has still got to be sold to a small market which becomes a mass market for it to be really successful. When thinking up a twist on something that already exists, the existing product is already known in the market place and therefore doesn't require such a leap in understanding.

What you may like to stop and think about for a moment is whether you believe this concept to be true for you? Whereas you may fully accept that the human imagination is a valuable commodity, it's like agreeing that selling iPhones is likely to make you a lot of money, but you just don't happen to be in the iPhone business yourself. The key to making this work is to be able to convince yourself of two things. Firstly, that you are imaginative and creative and secondly, that there is value in your head.

Some years ago I was watching a documentary about app designers in Las Vegas who were initially raising money to create new applications for technology. What astonished me was the amounts of money being asked for from seed capital type investors. The other part of the surprise was the fact that they were actually getting the sums they asked for. Furthermore, some of the ideas were far from creative or inventive, and yet the designers ended up being able to make their application holding the lion's share of the final product as it went to market.

You may wish to consider the fact that the world has a massively growing appetite for new content, material and ideas. If you consider the film and television industry, they require a great deal of content. What's fascinating is that because the majority of people don't feel they have any ideas to contribute, the people that do invariably sell quite basic and not that mind-blowing ideas. There are after all no new ideas but twists, re-hashes and re-spun offerings from old ideas. That's why we see so many re-makes of films and TV shows of yesteryear.

CONSIDERATION THREE:
SELLING THE MOST SUCCESSFUL PRODUCT OF ALL TIME

Though we've discussed content, I wanted to keep this type of content separate as a concept because it deserves it's own accolade. It's the story. Since cavemen days, the story has been one of the most popular products ever. Stories capture the imagination and attention of humans and will always do so.

Whether you are creating a tangible home appliance product, an app, a car, a holiday or a new type of aircraft, the real selling can only start when there's a story in place, even if the story is part of a short advertising campaign.

The story is a massive money concept. Look at what you're doing and what you sell. If you have a regular job with an employer you are selling your time, therefore selling yourself. What is your story? The reason it's important to know this is for promotion purposes, particularly if you decide to leave your employer and go for an interview elsewhere. Whatever the case you will need a powerful story to get attention. This could be about your values and how with your experience what you're able to contribute in the future.

It's often said that everyone has a book inside them. I would go along with this. No matter who you are there is an original story that lives within you. Find a way of using it, and you will be activating something of value that at the moment lies dormant.

This also goes for creating a proper story around any product you have invented or are currently selling. If you have a website, what's the story there? When you meet someone or network do you have a one-liner which starts your story off?

There's something very magnetic about a personal story. If you're about to address a group of people, say for example a product presentation. You're more likely to get a positive response if the people in the room know something about you. It's the reason why so many people around the world love watching soap operas on television. We are intrigued about faces and what lies behind each face. In other words what's their story? Start to think, 'What's the story?' As often as you can, with as many things you can, and dig up some 'gold' that can add value to you and/or what you're selling.

CONSIDERATION FOUR: HAVE A PERSONAL BLUEPRINT

If you're running a business the chances are you will have a blueprint to work from, in other words a business plan. Having said this, I am astounded at the number of small to medium sized businesses that decided they don't need any kind of plan and I call such businesses working *in their businesses* rather than *on their businesses*. The first is being entirely operational where the second is being much more strategic.

If you accept that every business should have a business plan and know where they are going, why do we not apply this to ourselves given that we as individuals are 'a business' in our own right? We need PR, a 'shop window' to the world, need to market ourselves in our careers, certainly need a 'financial department' as well as leadership and be aware of customer care needs (our partner, children etc). Yes, you are a business! Therefore what's your blueprint? Such a document isn't for the world to see and is usually for your eyes only, but it should contain a kind of personal business plan for the future. Both words and figures. Having a blue print makes it abundantly clear to both your conscious and sub-conscious mind where you're headed and why. Reading through it once a month will either make you pleased with your progress or a need to make some small (or large) changes to the strategy. When you come to the 'Hands' section of this book, you'll be shown how to create this simple document quite quickly.

CONSIDERATION FIVE:
LACK OF GRATITUDE BRINGS A POVERTY MINDSET

If you believe in God and pray regularly, the chances are you will be thankful for everything you have and whether you are religious or not, this is such a useful way to remind yourself that you are not poor, certainly in terms of your mindset. Having a poor or 'poverty' mindset means that invariably you're looking at what's wrong with your life and never what's right and in fact needs celebrating. An easy and down-to-earth way of showing gratitude, is starting a gratitude diary. At the end of the day you write down everything that you are grateful for. This could be on a day when you had all sorts of unfortunate things happen, yet you deselect the bad and underline and record the good.

It can be very cathartic and regularly give you a much more positive mindset. I have also noticed that you become more aware of the good things that happen to you every day because your mind is already thinking of creating a diary note for it! Just imagine this one idea will make you enjoy life more than you are currently…

You should also extend this to other people if you want to be 'mindset richer'. Thanking people and showing them gratitude for some of the smaller things that can easily be overlooked has the most momentous effect both on those you are communicating with and of course yourself. This concept is ridiculously simple to activate and sustain. I remember making the suggestion to a friend once. When he heard the idea he absolutely loved it and told me he would be putting this into practice immediately. Some weeks later when I asked him how he was getting on with his gratitude diary, I could not believe his response.

He said that he had not yet started it because when he went out to look for one he couldn't find a suitable journal to buy! Clearly, at a subconscious level he has no intention of doing this, which is a real shame because there really is no excuse. Find something to write on, plus something to write with, place these items near your bed, use them every day, minimum single line entry per day, job done.

CONSIDERATION SIX: CHANGE THE MENTAL RECORD

We all probably have a broken record playing in our head about money and our relationship with it. For some it's a great piece of music which enriches us and leads us to new opportunities, which in turn brings in more money as we listen to the tune once more. It's clear that the majority of people have a record that is out of tune and sounds rather negative and pessimistic.

There are also those who never allow themselves to have money and have created a self-imposed barrier to where they want to ultimately be. So as a result of the broken record this is unlikely to ever happen. The way to change your record is to first of all acknowledge that you have one in your head.

This is probably the most difficult thing to do because as you listen you hear nothing. Of course this isn't a real piece of music rather a constant self-talk voice which may only be heard subconsciously. One of the most challenging things to do with self-talk is to get rid of it. In using the analogy of changing the record, once you catch yourself saying negatives about your financial future, simply tell your inner voice to 'Shut Up'. As ridiculous as this may sound, this does in fact work and there is nothing lost in giving this a go. I will be covering other ideas, so for now let's move on to the next concept.

CONSIDERATION SEVEN: HOW RICH ARE YOU ALREADY?

When you read the title of this concept, I bet you anything you like, you immediately thought of money. However this has nothing to do with money, yet everything to do with wealth. I'd like you to grab a pen and paper and write down a long list of everything you currently have which you deem to be extremely important in your life, yet these same things you would be unable to buy with any form of cash. For example; a fantastic family, an amazing partner, beautiful children, food, clothing and shelter, regular income, a riveting hobby, some wonderful friends, evenings in by a log fire. You must define what these are and keep writing, because the longer the list you're able to create the richer you really are.

Though similar to the gratitude diary, the difference with this is that you are tallying up everything of value in your life that on the whole money cannot buy. Most of the items that you are now considering you would be unable to link with financial value. Imagine also the millions of people around the world who do not have all these items and sadly a few may have none of these items. Compared with them you are a kind of billionaire.

When you're your done with your list, keep it somewhere and review it every so often. Do add to it and keep reminding yourself of how life has smiled upon you already, and will continue to do so if you are able to ask for what you want in a particular way that we are going to look at later.

CONSIDERATION EIGHT: THE 3 TOP LAWS OF 'RICH' PEOPLE

I have read many lists of laws pertaining to people with considerable tangible wealth. I would like to distil all this information into three laws for your consideration, because these three things you could do or be aware of with relative ease. They are not difficult and simply require some application. However, I do know that anyone who has tangible wealth <u>will</u> be doing all these three things all the time. I know we discussed the fact that there is now two types of wealth to consider. The money variety and the non-money variety. So I'm not suggesting we refocus our efforts on the former.

Remember that money will always follow the right actions. Money rarely follows people who focus on it and nothing else. So here are the three laws:

1:SAVE FIRST: When you get your hands on money, save part of it first and then decide how you will spend the rest, not the other way around.

2:YOU ARE THE WEALTH: Remember that you are the most important aspect for future wealth of either variety. In short you are the money. What you think about and what actions you take as a result will lead to outcomes. If the outcomes are not desired outcomes then change the thoughts and actions.

3:EXPECT IT: Never look for money, expect it. However, expect the thing that will bring you money as a result on your success. So for example, think about adding value, doing more for your employer or a customer (going the extra mile). So expecting positive feedback, a pat on the back, a promotion or more business as a result of your great standards of excellence is the way to go.

CONSIDERATION NINE:
DECIDE ON YOUR DEFINITION OF 'WEALTH'

This is a really important one. What is your very own definition of wealth in your life? For example, if you could live on £1500 per month and this will give you tremendous pleasure, it means that by focusing on attracting approximately £20,000 a year you could consider yourself wealthy! Equally, if have a genuine desire for a lot more things going on around you, which you value important in your life, and would equate to £150,000 a year, then any blueprint you have or focus you need to bring into play needs to take account of this.

The majority of people can clarify what they want to do with their lives simply by spending a little time working it out. The surprise is that often they need a lot less than they expect. What a great exercise this is, to sit down and truly workout the minimum (comfortable) sum that you need to create monthly or annually to be happier with more time and freer to do more things of your choosing.

CONSIDERATION TEN: HAVE A COMPELLING VISION

One of the hardest things to derail or stop is a man or woman with a compelling vision. We often refer to them as "a person on a mission"! There are very few people who have one by the way, yet those that do, are unstoppable and invariably get exactly what they perceive in their minds eye. In business, having a vision is discussed quite a lot, however if you are going to have a vision it needs to be a compelling one. When you have a compelling vision you need less self-motivation because the very thought in your head propels you forward. Secondly you have something to share with other people who may be able to help you with the idea, and if the compelling vision is to do with a product you want to sell, you have a much better chance to be successful because customers will get to understand it quickly.

One of Stephen Spielberg's film successes is the movie *Jaws* from 1973. He apparently had major challenges making this movie, and there was a point at which he really thought it was not going to happen.

Fortunately, it was completed and is one of the most successful movies of its genre of all time. Probably the thing that saved it was Spielberg's unstoppable compelling vision that took him through the tough times and pushed both himself and the project across the finishing line. What you may wish to nip in the bud here and now is not having a compelling vision. Living a life without one is accepting mediocrity.

When you choose to live in mediocrity unless it's exactly what you want through design, then you are giving up the chance for the things we've already expressed like freedom, more time, quality living and happiness.

The best way to create a compelling vision is to start by thinking of all the big goals you may wish to achieve in your lifetime. Ultimately, work out what one thing needs to be the next thing and possibly the only thing you need to achieve success. Having identified the item, you now need to work out what the compelling part of it is or could be. For example your big goal may be to live and work in a sunshine climate. That in itself is a perhaps a great vision for you, but the compelling part is about what it would lead to, what it could bring to you and your family and the fact that on paper this move is more than feasible. So a compelling vision is a goal that has been thought through in detail and the key aspect of it identified which motivates and inspires action and the desire for achievement.

10 Considerations Summary

Now you have seen these 10 concepts, decide which ones you want to use/act on. I would like to suggest that you answer this question first:

"How serious are you about changing your fortune for the better in a big way?"

Before you answer this I'd like to tell you about a friend of mine who is able to stop people from smoking. He uses psychology, and it's very effective. However, he has to interview people before he can help them. The first question is, "Why do you want to stop smoking?" As he listens to the answer he watches body language while trying to pick up visual clues as to whether they are being honest and open.

After making a mental note of their answer he asks a 'killer question', which is, "Give me a score out of 10, 10 being high of how important it is for you to stop smoking". If it is nine or less, he reluctantly explains that he is unable to help them. Only people who score 10 have any chance of his technique working on them.

So now going back to my question, how serious are you and what score would you give out of 10?

If you score 9 or less, the rest of this book should be an interesting read and will be very useful to you. However, I would be unable to guarantee success. If however your score is 10, then you clearly are serious and should work on all 10 of the money concepts, because anything less than this will not be so helpful or efficacious.

Starting a New Journey with Money

In a moment you need to take a journey into your future. Imagine if you will, a few years into the future. It starts with you getting up one morning. But the difference here is that you are getting up in your dream home. Using your mind's eye imagine the bedroom. How large is it? What does it overlook? Take a wander into the hallway and to your ideal bathroom. Check out the fixtures and fittings. Also what's the rest of the house like? Walk through the various rooms, then out to the garage and the car you drive. How are you feeling today? And where are you headed? What sort of work do you do? And how are the other members of your family occupied? Do they work or have their own businesses? Now think about your next planned holiday in your world of the future. What have you booked? How excited are you about going there? What are your hobbies and pastimes? Seriously think through all of this…

It's curious when people are asked to think about their future. A few will create the most elaborate lives full of opulence and wealth, a large number will be content with an above average lifestyle and moderate riches, while a sizeable chunk of people will find the whole thing either ridiculous or a completely impossible task.

If you found this exercise easy and enjoyable, then you either have a good relationship with money, or you are mystified why you find it tough to have the quantity you desire. If on the other hand you can't imagine a wealthy you in the future then you have equal challenges around the topic of money. Whichever camp you currently sit in, you probably need to take a journey of discovery around money that opens your mind to new possibilities.

Not all of us actually want unlimited riches remember and I do want you to always consider money and wealth in the alternative context throughout this book when we use the terms *money* and *wealth*. The alternative is seeing the freedom that money brings as far more important. As your 'Money Guide', it's not for me to push you in any single direction. Suffice to say, that this book may be just what you need to really take stock of your current financial situation and allow you to re-shape it in a way that gets you closer to how you would like it to be. After all, if money was like air and you had excessive amounts of it in your life, this book would surely be an unlikely title for you to be reading.

Of the many aspects we'll be exploring, one key factor that will emerge again and again is all about your relationship with money. If Money was an individual who lived and breathed yet was the epitome of what money means to us all, then would it be a friend of yours or a long lost relative? Are you comfortable in Money's company or does Money unnerve you? Maybe you avoid Money whenever you can and are afraid to look Money directly in the face. Perhaps over the years your relationship with Money has deteriorated? It all started out well, but perhaps you feel let down, even betrayed and as a result don't have much to say about this being in your life who you seem to need, yet it doesn't feel a reciprocal thing at all.

If there's one thing that absolutely needs to happen as a result of exploring Money though the pages of this book, it's you getting closer to Money and improving your relationship with it.

Time and time again, people who explore who Money is and what Money is capable of, realise that those of us who have a great relationship with this entity at some point in their lives decided to change the relationship. Curiously there are many who do not value their connection with it and even disrespect their relationship.

Either now or shortly, you will need to think hard about your current money relationship, and if it's not as you would like it to be, would you be prepared to open your mind, and if need be, radically change the relationship? Money has been at the heart of most of my business life. Helping people to value it more, safeguard their future, better plan the major money needs of their life and helping them find appropriate ways of increasing the amount they had through saving and ultimately investments. But the area I used to overlook, mainly because my profession didn't include it as part of the overall offering was *how to get more money*. Once I began to ask the questions: 'What amount of money do you need in your life?' and 'Would you like to have more money in your life?' the response was so overwhelming, that I decided to sit down and give this aspect some serious consideration.

Most money professionals have very little to say about *growing more money* probably because it appears to be such a vast nebulous subject or that it's not within their remit. Yet if you really think about it, there are some very basic principles at work that people who are good with money use the world over that can and should be shared.

If you want more money in your life in a realistic and achievable way that's not all based on metaphysics, *Growing Your Own Money* will potentially help you set a new and exciting financial horizon. To begin with, it's worth thinking about six key 'money conversations'. These ideas have been gleaned over the years and have contributed to scores of people sufficiently changing their financial goals direction enough to make a significant impact on their ultimate destination.

KEY MONEY STRATEGIES

The Difference between:

Making Money and Making 'The Right Amount' of Money

In a book about money, perhaps there's little surprise in choosing to mention that famous Dickensian quotation spoken by one Mr. Micawber:

"Annual income twenty pounds, annual expenditure nineteen [pounds] nineteen [shillings] and six [pence], result happiness. Annual income twenty pounds, annual expenditure twenty pounds and six, result misery."

This is the primary money concept in its simplest form. An excess (of income over expenditure) creates happiness and a lack of it misery. Such a concept hasn't changed since money became the way we do business, acquire or sell goods and interact with each other on planet earth.

This book is about evening out the curves that all of us have to contend with in our financial lifetimes, yet more than this, it's about being able to *build, create and attract money* with integrity in a way that matches who you are, or more importantly perhaps, who you want to be. It's not about financial advice as such, but hopefully one read through will give you scores of highly inspirational ideas that could transform your finances for the better - perhaps beyond your previous hopes and dreams.

People who are born into money have a completely different relationship with money compared to those who are born into poverty and a lack of money. This sounds obvious, yet when you think about it, it should make no difference in theory. All babies learn at a tender age that water is wet. Whether you are rich or poor your relationship with wetness is universally accepted by all. Money however isn't as straight forward.

Rich children are usually given a great deal of 'coaching' on the value money brings and how to keep more and spend less. The poor child however is soon led to understand from experience and accept that money is a scarce commodity and extraordinarily difficult to acquire let alone keep. In short, that life ahead is probably going to be difficult. It's therefore easy for the rich child and poor child to have a similar shared vision that having as much of it as possible is a good thing and the way a successful life works.

So, one's life is about making as much money as you can with the intention of building your supply of it whether you do or do not need to and that money considerations are more important than any other. This leads to billionaires always looking for the next billion rather than enjoying what they have. Recently billionaires like Bill Gates have decided to give away most of their wealth which is impressive and admirable. The majority of rich people however rarely think this way, almost as if they are going to live forever, or worse, that they can take it with them when they die.

If someone came up to you right now with a magic cheque book and asked you: 'How much money would you like?', would you know the sum you'd ask for? But what if there was a catch? If you stated a sum that was in excess of your real needs or a sum that would not meet your real needs, the cheque could not be cashed! (Only a sum give or take a 5% margin of error would be cashable). So, do you know what this amount is? Most people have no idea, and the reason is that they've never worked it out. It's like going into a restaurant and complaining about the food *before* you've actually chosen the items you want from the menu. It makes no sense whatsoever.

Before you go any further, start to work out your true requirements. Things that would genuinely make you happy, but avoid asking for anything that you think you're supposed to ask for. It's easy to think of owning a luxury yacht, but seriously, is this something you continually daydream about?

Using Money 'Laws'

Sadly in most major cities today there are poor people sleeping on the streets. There will be some who do it purely by choice because it's a business almost, but the vast majority clearly do have a major financial black hole in their lives and they are reduced to begging in order to survive.

It can be heart wrenching when children are involved and like me it leaves you thinking the question: 'How can I help more long term and significantly beyond simply giving them some one-time money?' Whether you are begging for money or 'asking the universe to provide' in a more metaphysical way, there is one major fallacy that's always overlooked. It's... what are you prepared to offer, give or to do in return?

The act of not asking what you will offer in return first is the reason so many people find the 'Law of Attraction' not working the way they were led to believe. You may believe in something for nothing, but I have yet to prove there is such a thing. Despite the Law of Attraction seeming to suggest if you think it enough you attract it, good or bad, thinking up front what you would want to offer in return might make it sit within your subconscious more easily, making the process more likely to work.

Equally, if beggars in the street were offering something in return for the money they were requesting, again they are much more likely to get something. It follows a very simple law, more potent than 'The Law of Attraction' called *The Law of Reciprocity*. What you give someone you will invariably get back in one form or another. Reciprocation is overlooked all too often, and is relatively easy to deploy in life. Don't think of the money or item you want on its own without stating what you'd be prepared to do in exchange first. In working out the exact sum you want if there was a magic cheque book, now ensure you also know how you intend to get the sum by offering back value in exchange.

If you wanted to also use affirmations to attract money, simply saying: 'I want more money' is unlikely to get lots of money flying in your direction all of a sudden.

However if you stated: 'Since launching my amazing online business the money flow is more than I ever dreamed possible…' then you are more likely to achieve it because you are telling your mind that you already have it and it needs to catch up. With this in mind and what's happening in the world in general, could creating money today have become easier?

In the past 20 years, the internet has transformed the way we live our lives and how we do business. What is possible today in your spare time online was not an option two decades ago. And there are still scores of alternative opportunities which are off line. More than ever before, age, sex, culture are no longer considerations. We are able to outsource everything, even getting someone else to come up with the idea for us to use and work on.

THE WEALTHY MINDSET

Do you want to make a marginal gain in your finances or go for a serious transformation? This rather depends on what you want money to do for you. I remember a couple of friends working out to the exact penny how much money they would have to suddenly acquire to be able to have, be and do everything they dreamed of acquiring. What is interesting is that they go through this exercise every year, and what is thought provoking is the fact that the amount seems to be getting smaller! As they get older they realise what they would be happy with is not as much as they first imagined. That his and hers sports car that would cost £250,000 has now vanished off the list four years later, and the requirement of £15,000 income a month (each) has been cut down in size by 66% (each). At the same time they have noticed that their overall standard of living has risen and they are happier now compared with four years ago.

The learning here for them is that by working out what you want and then reviewing it in time, the gloss of fast cars and mega rich properties has lost its tarnish and the much smaller sum they would like to make a reality is also looking exceedingly more possible.

The process of coming up with a figure however was a form of using the Law of Attraction, and I am convinced this did have something to do with the lowering of their requirements while improving the feeling around what they do already have and what they need in reality in the future.

Imagine a 'genie' popping out of a bottle with a cheque book and saying to you: Name your figure and it's yours. However, the proviso is that the genie needed to see a list of everything priced up including regular income wants… I have to assume you would not get a cheque because you like the vast majority simply do not know an exact amount.

So here's the point. If you don't know that figure, neither does your sub-conscious; that simply follows your instructions to the letter and is programmed to believe that in this case it can't be that important. This in turn means it does no work in sending you great ideas that may help you towards goals and dreams - because they are still to be priced up!

Incidentally, the couple in their mid 50s started with a requirement of £8,865,462 four years ago, and today the sum is a much smaller £1,229,117.

OBTAINING MORE MONEY QUICKLY

Money can be created quite quickly and most certainly doesn't have to be a laborious process that takes years. Fast cash however does have 3 factors you need to be aware of.

1 - Fast money normally would necessitate some sort of selling.

2 - Whatever you decide to sell should be thought about carefully. For example it's easier to sell encrypt-able memory sticks for computers today than pads and pens.

3 - Add Value. Whatever you are selling, your customer needs to see additional value by coming to you rather than going elsewhere. If you work out a good added value proposition along with great service and keen pricing, money can come in quite quickly.

In summary: Right product, tick. Good Price, tick. And what's the added benefit of dealing with you?

Fast cash can also come about without products but choosing services. Two people decided to offer visitors in their town a bed for the night very cheaply to include breakfast, however using air beds. The idea was logged and caught on eventually culminating in airbnb.com. What's interesting it that it started out as air beds and now it included an entire house that you can rent out.

Someone else I know of started a shopping service for residents in her locality. It went down a storm and she started to make money, but unfortunately she didn't have the resources or support to make it into a really viable business. Dog-walking services too have been created by people realising that there is a big economy to be exploited.

The next form of fast cash is undoubtedly there right now waiting for someone to recognise the potential. Maybe there is something that you could discover by simply alerting your subconscious of the fact?

The UK TV Game Show 'Deal or No Deal' was pitched to 8 different companies before it was taken up. Now it's become the most successful TV game show in the world. Prior to this Alfred Hitchcock's famous blockbuster *Psycho* was also rejected several times and the director had to finance the movie personally in order to get it made. These two stories are examples of persistence and mindset.

For those of us who are prepared to go the distance and never give up, we are likely to be successful in our endeavours where others may even be jealous. Those that roll over and die at the first hurdle rarely attain what their minds wish for in their lives and these same principles certainly apply to the attraction and creation of money. It's not about wanting money for itself, but having a purpose you've identified together with a detailed plan of how you intend to attain it.

TESTING YOUR WEALTH/POVERTY MINDSET

Try this simple quiz making a note of the 10 scores which becomes an overall percentage score. Don't think too much about your answer, just go with what feels the right score. Agreement with the statement scores low and disagreement scores high - all out of 10.

Here we go:

Q1: My gut feeling tells me that I am not destined to be very wealthy

Q2: I am more comfortable in a regular job versus running my own business/practice

Q3: You cannot create more money by attaining a more positive mindset

Q4: People who are rich were invariably born into money

Q5: If you are born rich it's easier to create more wealth than if you are born poor

Q6: Money is the root of all evil

Q7: I would find it embarrassing to suddenly become more wealthy

Q8: Money is difficult to make outside a regular job

Q9: Making more money needs a great deal of skill

Q10: Making more money requires a great deal of specialised knowledge

YOUR RELATIONSHIP WITH MONEY: INTERPRETATION

0-11 You have some real money issues that need dealing with. Probably the biggest factor standing in your way is yourself. That and your core beliefs about money which have been passed on to you by family, friends, the media and possibly school. There is a way forward provided you are prepared to truly open your mind. Try this quiz after you read the book. If your score is the same, then the answer lies in changing your negative beliefs. (We tell you how).

11-20 The chances are you have had a challenging time with money to date, in particular whilst growing up. Somewhere along the line you've decided that your experiences to date equate with the future which of course is not necessarily the case. Give this book a quick read through, then go through it a second time and make notes. Come away with half a dozen significant ideas and put them into action. This is your route forward.

21-30 Not a great score but a hopeful one. There is sufficient doubt in your mind for you to try something new and different. You need a new approach and attitude towards money. Make a decision to change and become more positive minded on the subject and things could look very different in a year from now. Though a low score, see this as life pointing you now in a new and potentially very exciting direction.

31-40 It would be interesting to know whether all your scores were similar or did you in fact have some quite high scores? If the latter, take a good look at these high scores and know that there are some positive windows of opportunity staring you in the face. If however your scores were pretty much the same across the board, yes you have a less positive than desired relationship with money, but one that most certainly can be improved if you can identify a desire and or purpose for a better level of personal wealth.

41-50 Almost the mid-way mark, but this in itself can mean that you are in two minds about money. Partly lacking confidence about improving your relationship with money, partly knowing instinctively that you are capable of making a big turn towards a better financial future. Read this book completely and then make a firm commitment to try a new approach perhaps?

51-60 You are officially above the average score and pointing in the right direction. This is a good place to be, and if you bought this book yourself it shows you have come to a point in your life where you know that something serious needs to be done if you are going to change your future fortunes for the good. As an additional check, what score would you give yourself for *your* desire to change/do something new and different to improve your finances? Any score above 50 bodes well. Below 50 and you need to work on your self belief and self confidence first. We tell you how in the book.

61-70 This is an interesting score area because though it's well above average, the chances are that you scored quite low on a couple of questions. This means you do have money mindset issues, but ones that can be dealt with provided you are prepared to really put some effort behind your actions. It's unlikely that you have a sound financial position. If you do have one, then you are probably on a plateau and need a push. If you lack a sound financial position which is more likely, then one of the goals from reading this book is to take a couple of ideas and do your utmost to make them work. Once you do, there will be nothing to stop you. You are probably the kind of person who needs hard evidence before you make any changes.

71-80 A very good score, so you should feel proud of your money mindset. And as you read this, there is probably a little voice in your head saying something to counter any positivity. For you, this is the key to making any transformation possible. You have a sufficiently positive relationship with money, but your challenge is the link between this and the belief yourself. Fix the latter part and you've fixed the bigger picture - then nothing will hold you back.

81-90 This is indeed a high wealth mindset score and the world is your oyster! The challenge you have is that you do doubt yourself occasionally which makes you stop and think - reflect even. If you're young, fine. But if you are over 50 then you don't have the luxury of time on your side and need to make some decisions now and complete your plans.

91-100 You have the perfect wealth mindset which suggests you are already doing well financially or have the mental agility to turn the corner immediately if you choose to do so.

How to Get the Best from the Rest of this Book

One unfortunate habit we have in being Human is that we can easily get distracted. Life itself has so many things to take us off in various directions, often when we are unaware of the diversion. How many self help books have you ever read, or articles you've seen or TV programmes you've watched where at the time you were excited, even exhilarated and wanted to follow through on the ideas presented, only to find a few days later you could hardly remember what exactly you did experience.

It's going to be such a waste of time reading this book that has been designed to help you to grow much more money in your life to the level you genuinely need if after reading it you simply go back to the point at which you started and nothing has changed.

This is why there's an ACTION NOTES page after each chapter for you to make a note in and commit to linked actions. It will make it much easier to review the book, and having committed sacrilege in writing in a book, it will also make you feel this is a work-book rather than a theoretical take-no-action textbook.

You may also consider finding a like minded soul to buddy up with. This would allow discussion, personal commitment and ensuring you are both on track. The other option is to get yourself a life coach to support you. Make sure you choose wisely and only go this route if you know that you are the type of person who can easily allow things to slide.

Character Notes and Steps

WHAT ARE THE MOST IMPORTANT MESSAGES?

ACTION IDEAS

ACTION STEPS – *MY COMMITMENT*

2

Significant Money Facts

"Those who are easily shocked should be shocked more often."
Mae West

1 - THE POWER OF TIME

I can never remember learning about time in a lesson at school, other than in maths and physics classes as a medium of measurement. Yet it is such an important topic where money and wealth is concerned. If school children were given pension advice and they were to start putting money away at 18, just imagine how well off everyone would be at age 60, or even 50.

Consider a sum which is quite trivial for most people in savings terms. Imagine you were to save just £5 per week into a savings account with a 3% return.

Over five years this amounts to £1,300 and with compound interest at 3% it's £1,402.13. So now let's look what happens over 40 years.

In 40 years you will have saved £10,400.

With 3% compound interest this becomes £20,097.73

Twice the principal at £10 per week?

In 40 years you will have saved £20,800.

With 3% compound interest this becomes £40,195.45

I often advise saving 10% of all your annual income if at all possible, though some financial advisers suggest this is not enough if you want to retire much earlier. However, if you were to calculate someone saving 10% of their income based on £30,000 today, the figure jumps to £226,203, yet over 40 years their income would hopefully increase considerably. So let's imagine we factor in a gentle rise in income at 2.5% per year, we then arrive at £346,184.

Finally, someone saving more seriously at £6,000 per year plus additional periodic lump sums totaling £150,000 over the 40 year period, based on some small financial projects or a very modest second business, and you would achieve £948,959!

If you think about it, this sum would become ten or twenty times greater because each year the individual could review the factors involved and what they were able to contribute taking into account the following:

- their income amount
- their additional lump sum capability
- interest rates
- inflation rates

The big catalyst factor here is time. Time is also a money creation catalyst in property, fine art, antiques and wine. Even certain toys have become collectors items and increased in value over 40 years. In the USA, the original Gameboy toy is now selling for around $850, a first generation Pokemon card at $649 and a cabbage patch doll, for $1,250.

One of the major recommendations I make in this book is that you create a blueprint for your money. Grab some paper, a calculator and access to a compound interest calculator on line and above all make a start. Being young has many advantages. Saving and investing money… growing it for the future is one major form of financial leverage that may be applied well by the under 30s. If you don't have youth on your side, don't worry there are plenty of other things to consider coming up.

2 - WEALTH IS A HABIT

This ties in well with making wealth a habit. Saving is purely a habit and there are two forms. Regular and spontaneous. What helps is an easy way to syphon off surplus money. Many would say that there is no 'surplus' money, but we know this is not the case. When something goes up like interest rates, fuel or energy prices people always find the money. So consider paying yourself first more often. Having a savings account with a plastic card could be one way to go. This means going into a well known bank when you are passing and adding to an account in your name which is also getting sums via a regular banker's order (or more than one).

To really make wealth a habit, you should be focused and aware of it on a day by day basis. Rather than thinking of what to purchase, think first each day of how much you could save today. What a great thing to do that you could link to brushing your teeth… today, how far could I go in paying myself something into my savings account? This won't be the first time I shall be saying this, just think about it. By having a savings account where you have no idea how much you are putting into it would be more effective that knowing on a day by day basis, or even seeing a monthly statement. Other healthy-wealthy habits include being aware of anything you could potentially sell that you are no longer using. Are there things you can dig out that could go to an auction? What about having a latest wealth creation project on the go? This could be online related, creative, (books, blogs, painting, craft work, YouTube), or be around something you are selling or re-selling.

It's a stark fact that people with money think about acquisition in some form infinitely more often than the majority who think about money disposal in one form or another more often.

3 - RETIRE EARLY. VERY EARLY

So when do you want to retire?

I would like to separate this question from the sociological one of whether it should be early or even never. My suggestion is to consider this as less about retirement, but unleashing some financial independence into your life. With this in mind, then you should be thinking sooner rather than later. More and more Millennials seem to be looking for short cuts to a long work-free life. Worst case, working and enjoying every minute of it. Like for example the blogger and vlogger (video blogger) revolution on sites like YouTube. Some young people in particular seem to be doing well attracting lots of subscribers which in turn attract advertisers and a revenue stream. The downside is content and holding on to your audience not to mention plenty of healthy competition vying for the same audience.

Assuming we side step these possibilities for an early retirement, then we should seriously consider how anyone can plan for a very early retirement. When I say very early, I am suggesting from age 40, but to be fair on the younger readers I need to cover off the following three possibilities.

20-30

Anyone in this category who can 'stop' at 30 has definitely hit the big time.

- singers
- screen writers
- actors, dancers
- young entrepreneurs (often in technology)
- original business ideas
- other media related success

If you are not in one of these categories and you haven't come into an unexpected windfall then it's likely you need to work on a little longer.

30-40

The number of people finding ways of saying "time out" compared to having to work regularly are on the increase. They can be late starters from the first group, or they have just been shrewd in creating a twenty year blueprint which has worked out. To seriously have the chance to retire at 40 you will need to have accumulated sufficient money to take you potentially through a further 50 years of life. This could equate to a large lump of cash of course. The type of situations for a 'Retire at 40' ticket holder would be most likely someone who has started a business, potentially licensed or franchised it, and either is able to live from the annual income or sell their share for a very large sum.

When I was in my late 20's I made a conscious decision and created a life plan to aim to be able to have the choice to retire by the time I reached age 40. The way I did this was to combine all the ideas of saving and investing money, developing and growing my business along with keeping control of the income and expenditure principles that I've shared. On reaching age 40 I'd already received two offers to sell the business which would easily have put me in a place where (should I have chosen to), I could have retired. My decision so far has been to continue mainly due to the fact that I'm having so much fun, my children are young and tied to school and I genuinely enjoy helping people get to where they want to be in terms of life and financial goals too. Its great to have the choice and it's great to help put people in a place where they have a choice too!

40-55

This area of possibility is within everyone's reach provided you have a good 20 years plus run of time on your side. If you have not got so long then keep reading. A half decent pension scheme taken out early enough and supplemented with lump sums should put you in a very good position to have a regular cheque coming your way from your 50th birthday. If you have a small additional income based on creating a small business too, you would be in good shape.

THE HARD FACTS ABOUT RETIRING EARLY

What it all boils down to is knowing what your disposable income is each month. Very few people ever know this 'combination to your personal future money safe'. Quite simply…

Monthly Income-Monthly Expenditure=Disposable Income

Let's say it's £2,500-£1,800 giving you £700 disposable monthly income which is £8,400 per year. This amount certainly will not allow you to retire in 10 years though it could in say 40 years provided inflation and additional lump sums were taken into account. The key then is to boost the disposable figure to as high as possible, and the easiest way would be to *reduce* monthly expenditure. However, here you have a dilemma. Do you save for the future and enjoy the present less, or enjoy the present and have less money when you retire? Most people go for the middle ground. So what percentage of your income would allow you to retire early? Assuming your savings interest rate is 5% then here is one school of thinking:

- Save 10% a year and you could retire 40-50 years
- Save 25% a year and you could retire after 32 years
- Save 50% a year and you could retire in 17 years
- Save 75% a year and you could retire in 7 years

There's little point going into the nitty gritty details of how anyone could even contemplate saving 75% of their income, though if you were making £10,000 per month or £120,000 a year net, then it could be very feasible.

An alternative school of thinking states that you actually need 23 times your current net income to contemplate retiring.

If you currently make £22,000 per year this equates to £506,000. If you are making £47,000 it would be £1,081,000. This of course takes into account staying with your current quality of life/lifestyle.

Yet when you place these two different schools of thought side by side, anyone making £22,000 would end up with either £115,500 (75% of £22,000 x 7) or £506,000 (£22,000 x 23). So ultimately you must make a judgment call based on working it out for yourself based on:

- how much you make at the moment
- how much you are prepared to live on with zero additional income
- how much more you could make in addition to 'up' the figures

Today at the time of writing this book, it is feasible to live on a modest annuity of £1,300 per month with a capital base of £250,000. At state retirement age, this would be supplemented by a government pension.

If none of this has inspired you, maybe you need to consider idea 4.

4 - TODAY IS THE BEST TIME EVER TO MAKE MONEY.

In the 1960s and 70s very few people compared to today started their own businesses. It would have required more capital and the mindset of the population was such that the entrepreneurial bug just had not caught on yet. It was the 1980s that brought a new 'money making fever wave' into life and lots of businesses were launched as well as crashed and burned. Largely however, the businesses were still 'old world' non-technology enterprises, and despite companies launched by the Steve Jobs and Bill Gates types, it wasn't really until the year 2000 that the average person could contemplate jumping on this bandwagon. We all remember the 'dot com bubble' and subsequent collapse, though that should not put people off today. Currently new technology businesses is on a rapid increase with the new kid on the block being *The Internet of Things*. This relates to the new trend of having intelligent machines - heaters, TVs, lighting, electrical equipment, security systems, cars that can all be controlled via your mobile device.

In my own business - financial services - I have opted to join the digital business revolution in co-creating a software development company called Decode Studios. I totally recognise the opportunity here and I am pleased to say that this business so far has been a good decision. The big plus is that I don't need technical knowledge or experience for it because I can outsource everything I need... and so can you.

The only thing that holds people back is fear. And there's nothing to be afraid of to investigate what's out there and what the possibilities are which is how I got involved in an industry that could have been a total mystery to me at the start.

Just for a peek at outsourcing in the most very basic sense, go to fiverr.com and look at what you can get for a few dollars… five dollars in fact. This may whet your appetite and get you buzzing.

Here's some other quick and simple 'money making advice':

- Form a Brain's Trust Collective. This is a group of people you trust and preferably each having a different skill to bring to the table. You share food and drink together *after* the session. You can debate your ideas, their suggestions, work out feasibility on potential projects, time investments, capital sums needed, projected returns and so on.
- Create your Blueprint for the way forward. Remember that this does not have to be a full blown business. It could be just an income stream.

As a quick aside, there was the story of the 'apps nerd' who had come up with a great little tool for the global market and nothing happened after three years. Not one sale. She then pitched the idea to a business Angels Consortium and they agreed to fund her 100% of the money she needed to make this into a small business in return for 49% of the shares. A deal was struck and a year later she was working from a small office with two full time programmers and a couple of support people. Her dating product is out there getting regular sign ups and subscriptions as well as good reviews.

- Start a PHOTO WALL of images that relate to your desired dream
- Tell a few people of your commitment and deadlines. Now, be careful here. This should only be applied if you are the type of person who would want to succeed if their reputation is on the line.
- Spend a Week-end with Google. Devote two full days of research on everything you can find on line that relates to your goal. Remember to also look at what may be on youtube.com which is becoming a very useful place to learn things. There are also additional low fee learning sites like udemy. com . This site can also be where you start your first business.
- Start. If you are not prepared to start and take some sort of action, then you might as well stop reading this and skip a few chapters. Even then I would be concerned on your behalf if you are not even prepared to investigate possibilities a bit further. There is of course another option. Read that book I mentioned, "How to Get Mega Rich While you Sleep and Wake up a Billionaire". Good luck with that.

Character Notes and Steps

WHAT ARE THE MOST IMPORTANT MESSAGES?

ACTION IDEAS

ACTION STEPS – *MY COMMITMENT*

3

It's Never Too Late to be Wealthy

We would accomplish many more things if we did not think them as impossible…
C. Malesherbes

Money comes second to a much more valuable resource - that of time itself. There is a point in your life when you will have run out of years to apply for a new mortgage for example, or start a pension for retirement, but does this apply to all things about money? Here's something to think about:

RAYMOND ALBERT "RAY" KROC

Kroc was an American businessman and bought into the McDonald's Brothers' Hamburger business in 1955 and built it into the most successful fast food operation in the world.

Kroc was featured in *Time 100*, the most important people in the century who had amassed a fortune during their lifetime. He even owned a well-known baseball team from 1974-1984 when he passed away. Similar to another fast-food giant KFC founder, Harland Saunders, Kroc's success came later in life when he was way past his 50th birthday.

It is certainly true that if you wanted to make a great deal of money in a relatively short space of time, you need to come up with something big, so yes the stakes are higher and require a bolder approach, but the end result can be more exciting than someone plodding away for 40 years and retiring on a 'get-by' pension. The key to the 'safe' is a strong mind-set and a decision to take *calculated* as opposed to *insane* risks. Kroc started his late spurt in the 1950s, but never before in the history of the world, have so many opportunities to make money been in so much abundance as they are today.

All it takes is a good idea, a small amount of seed capital which could be raised by the sale of shares and the guts to take action and see your idea through. It's also worth remembering the sad story of Ron Wayne a founder of Apple who is currently on state benefits today, who had an opportunity of a lifetime that he casually ditched for seemingly no significant reasoning.

Wayne worked with Steve Jobs at Atari before he, Jobs, and Wozniak founded Apple Computer on April 1, 1976. Serving as the venture's "adult supervision", Wayne drew the first Apple Logo, wrote the three men's original partnership agreement and wrote the first Apple manual. Wayne received a 10% stake in Apple but relinquished his equity for US $800 less than two weeks later, on April 12, 1976.

Legally, all members of a partnership are personally responsible for any debts incurred by any partner; unlike Jobs and Wozniak, then 21 and 25, Wayne had personal assets that potential creditors could seize. The failure of a company that he had started five years earlier also contributed to his decision to exit the partnership. Later that year, venture capitalist Arthur Rock helped develop a business plan and convert the partnership into a corporation.

A year after leaving Apple, Wayne received $1,500 for his agreement to forfeit any claims against the new company. In its first year of operations (1976), Apple's sales reached US$174,000. In 1977 sales rose to US$2.7 million, in 1978 to US$7.8 million, and in 1980 to US$117 million. By 1982 Apple had a billion dollars in annual sales.

In February 2015, Apple's value exceeded $700 billion, making it the most valuable U.S. Company by far. Had Wayne kept his 10% stock until then, it would have been worth approximately $60 billion.

Once more, having the guts to carry on is often what daunts people in later life. The young Steve Jobs was willing to risk it all (even though he didn't have that much to risk at the time), but the more considered Ron Wayne put on his 'sensible head' and made the wrong decision, all be it seemed the right thing to do at the time.

Some of the best ideas are probably going to emerge at a time you least expect it.

In 1984, a British technology graduate C.M. Fourman was driving to work when he thought about the concept of business contracts being signed on-line. At this time there was no facility or program to do this so he patented his idea even though he had not worked out the 'how-to' aspect yet. This was one of many ideas he had come up with for future technology design opportunities. Before he could wholly own the concept he had a final patent-related fee to pay of £300. Short of cash at the time, in that same week he had to fix his car for a similar sum and sadly allowed the patent to go by in favour of his transport. Though this sounds like another Ron Wayne story the salient points to note are…firstly, be prepared to 'receive' great ideas from your subconscious at any time, and when the idea comes through nail the idea to paper, or better still a notebook dedicated to your own great innovative thinking. Secondly, if you have a gut feeling about something, stay with it and see it through to at least the starting point.

A Rule of Thumb might be if time isn't on your side and you've never taken a reasonable risk to make a great deal of money in a very short time scale, don't you owe it to yourself to do so at least once in your life? Of course if you have a history of business failures and poor investments then it could be time to think of alternative ways forward, and inevitably there will be many options if you look hard enough.

A great way to really see the correlation between money and time is the following analogy. Just imagine that whenever you spent time you had to do so from writing a cheque from your time cheque book. So if you wanted to spend time at the shops you'd need to write a cheque for say three hours and thirty minutes. This time resource is then deducted from your master time bank account depleting your reserves, because you were credited with an unknown amount when the account was opened, and there is no way of crediting your time account. Each time you use it the time depletes until there's none left meaning the account is closed and your life is over. Think about how you would feel writing cheques from this account, particularly not knowing if the cheque you are writing will be the last one!

Such an analogy should make you appreciate time much more, and it's mentioned to allow you to answer the following question: "When you spend money rather than hang on to it do you feel the same way as in the time cheque book concept?" and "Do you value the money with the same significance?"

These sorts of questions and the time cheque book analogy is just the sort of thing that made my wife and I stop travelling to, walking round and purchasing our weekly supermarket shop. These days (and for some years now), our main weekly shopping is all done online and we even plan ahead and book a delivery when we're away on holiday in the UK. When you think about it we must have saved days if not weeks of time as a result and we now start our holiday off in the place that we've booked rather than spending an hour or two in the local supermarket!

Whatever age you are, there are always positive things you can do immediately to be better off. Here are ten tips, many of which I have shared with family, friends and clients.

MY TOP 10 GENERAL MONEY TIPS

1: 10% OF ALL I EARN IS MINE TO KEEP

In the days of liberal cheque-book use, this would have been a good slogan to have written on the front of your cheque-book. Even today, it can remind us that we tend to pay money out to everyone else yet rarely write a cheque to ourselves. A sobering exercise is to roughly workout how much money has passed through your hands from your first job to the present day. Now workout what the 10% figure is. Next look at a compound interest figure and then sit down before you collapse. Naturally the older you are the bigger the figure. This also has a lot to do with the interest you can get but 5% would allow you a fair assessment.

Apart from seriously considering teaching your children and grandchildren this slogan (of course teaching is one thing, getting them to do it is quite another), it appears much more challenging for adults to adopt the same measure. For those that do they will find they can get their habit in place within a few months before it becomes second nature.

There's an old story about Adam and Eve investing one penny. Adam opens an account which pays simple interest at 8% where Eve, who is a bit more shrewd opens an account where they pay 8% on a compound basis over say two thousand years. If we assume they lost their passbooks it would be interesting to note what their accounts would be worth today.

Adam's investment would be worth £1.51 and Eve would have a sum of money with 49 zeros! The moral here is to save regularly and ensure you benefit from compound interest or income.

The other analogy is imagining a new law that comes out all of a sudden. It states that every human being must pay 10% of what they receive from now on as a 'breathing tax'. If this were to really happen, and the alternative is to not be given the air to breathe, the chances are everyone would find the money regardless. If you really think about this setting aside 10% or a slightly smaller percentage, is a real possibility if you really decided upon it. It wouldn't take long before the effect of such disciplined savings would reflect very positively upon your finances.

So, what do you think? Would you be prepared to set aside a percentage you are comfortable with of all your income from now on? If you did this, what's the worst that could happen? Then consider what's the best that could happen?

2: Self Psychology Help

When people use credit cards, the reason they get into trouble is because they don't consider the card as being real money. If they were spending notes and coins the likelihood is that they would curb their spending or in fact not spend at all. For example, one debt counsellor suggested to a lady addicted to shopping that she should make cash withdrawals and then buy the goods rather than simply handing over her card at the counter. This apparently worked really well, even though she still felt she had to make purchases, however her overall shopping bill diminished by a staggering 71%. Some people have a personal agreement with themselves around spending and whatever they spend their money on which is a luxury item, they have to give three valid reasons in making a purchase.

These reasons are beyond things like simply, "I want it", "I like it" and "I have to have it". Many are pushed to come up with one good reason sometimes!

Alongside these ideas, there is the self-funding lottery account. This is about going mad on the lottery every week however paying all the funds into a separate account with your name on it. If you were to have done this over the last 20 years with interest, you'd have between £8-£12,000. Of course it's true that you may have won the Lottery and banked millions, yet the reality is that you are more likely to be struck by lightning. Someone once described the lottery as a tax on hope.

3: Open a Separate Spending Account.

Most people lose all track of their spending because they are 'losing money' as it were from various sources. Have you ever considered keeping a separate account purely for spending? This is very easy to set up and once you get into the habit of using a single financial source for spending it will immediately help you in the following way:

- tracking your spending
- identifying poor spending decisions more easily
- appreciating your true spending power at any time
- valuing the feeling of having money available to spend
- having a system to motivate you to save for your spending facility

Ideally your spending account should be with a different bank to your main personal account. (It's never a good idea to have one bank in life as they can hold you to account easily if you are having any financial challenges).

In terms of reviewing your spending, this is best done on a monthly basis. If you have the patience and this isn't for everyone, work out key spending areas on a pie chart. Such data can help guide you for next month's spending.

Some banks are doing this now for their customers. It is sobering to know that in a particular month you have spent £122 on cappuccino, £86 on the lottery and £93 on snacks. Whenever you see such information always reflect on alternative things you could have done with the money. The more you do this, the more chance you have of changing your money habits for the better.

The overall idea of having a spending account is about accountability, better planning and cutting down the 'holes in your pocket' where you may leak money indiscriminately or at least without any sensible reflection. The feeling a spending account promotes is a guilt-free association with controlled and considered spending. The spender is more relaxed and is therefore liable to better spend on what they really want.

4: Kill the Debt

Though we covered this earlier, it needs a little more consideration before we step away from it completely. In the 1980s it seemed fashionable to acquire lots of lines of credit. The theory behind this was very sound. Having 10 unused credit cards amounting to £70,000 as a facility overall is a sensible strategy provided it's there purely for emergency use. However this was in the 80s and it caught many people out because they were using the facility, not paying the balance off in full every month and apart from paying vast amounts of interest to the already rich card companies, they were falling into a spiral of debt. However, there is something to learn from being tempted into having credit cards or lines of credit. Banks love to lend to the rich and hate to offer anything to the less well off. So having credit when you don't need it can be a good thing, provided you are careful. Having said this, scores of big successful businesses today were started on credit.

One of the ways to eliminate debt is to be aware of it down to the last penny. For people who have debts, this is often the last thing they wish to do, but knowing where you are on a monthly basis, precisely worked out, is the first step to being able to 'look debt in the face' taking some strategic action to kill it.

As painful as it probably would be, equally important is having a single figure as to how much money you have parted with at the end of the year. It's actually all about engaging your subconscious mind so that it allows you to make better decisions about spending and debt in the future.

For those people who have many debt accounts, saving money to pay off each account one by one can be very cathartic. It's probably easier to start with the smallest account and work up and then change horses in mid-stream going for the biggest account and working down. The focus should really be on the account that is costing you the most in terms of the rate of interest payable and whether by overpaying you can reduce the overall interest that you will pay as the capital reduces.

The biggest challenge with debt reduction is that it can be a painful process both in knowing how much you have to deal with and the many pleasures you may need to forego in order to achieve your objective. Yet the fact of the matter is that no one who is able to remove all of their debt ever complains once they have attained that happy status.

Getting out of debt is probably a subject all of its own and there are many books out there that will help you further. Here as a money tip it's simply about having a strategy to deal with any debts you have rather than forgetting or ignoring them. Any serious debt will often do you no favours and will be set up to irritate and trouble you, causing you potential future hardship and significant regret.

5: NEVER PUT ALL YOUR EGGS IN A SINGLE BASKET.

Whereas this sounds like advice from your grandparents, in financial terms it is very sound thinking. There are so many ways you can distribute and channel your money that you may wish to consider a brainstorm session with a friend, colleague, accountant or financial adviser. Do some research and think wider than merely interest bearing accounts. Like for example partial or a full investment in property, a business, and shares in things that are already making money. There is always the risk element, yet overall if you make a profit then you are ahead of the game.

If you've ever watched *Dragon's Den* you'll know that the Dragon investors will invest in a number of businesses knowing full well that some will succeed and others won't. What they do know is that on balance they will win overall. There is no specific number of places you should consider and to some extent too many eggs can break the basket and create stress. Yet equally one single basket has broken the fortunes of many a business person and well known families over the centuries and should be avoided at all costs. Even distributing your money over different banks and savings companies is a better bet than simply having it all in one account.

6: Turning Junk into Cash

Many people use sites like Ebay to sell goods that they no longer want. It's a simple enough concept yet probably not for everyone.

This is mainly because of a lack of technical knowledge though this should not daunt you. If you potentially have lots to sell and monetise, then reading up on how to use Ebay or even going on a course may be a good investment for the future. It also gives you the opportunity to start your very own on-line business perhaps. Additionally there's the chance of turning up valuable items in your home that have been overlooked for years as simply 'junk'.

In a place called Elbow Lake, Minnesota USA, David Gonzalez bought a house that needed a lot of work for a mere $10,000. After completely demolishing a wall in the house he discovered that old comics in the Action Comic #1 series were used with newspapers as insulation. Action comics are the forerunner to arguably the most popular superhero of them all, namely Superman. Even though one of the comics wasn't in mint condition it was sold for $175,000, dwarfing the value of the house. Putting this into context, a near mint copy of Action Comics #1 owned by actor Nicolas Cage recently sold in an auction for $2.16 million in 2011.

In 2013, a Norwegian man discovered a painting in his attic by master painter Vincent Van Gogh. It was a previously unknown masterpiece of a landscape and sat there for years as he thought it was an obvious fake. The painting, *Sunset at Montmajour* therefore spent over one hundred years from public view. In 1991, the painting's then owners contacted the Van Gogh Museum in Amsterdam to get an opinion. It was immediately deemed a fake because it was unsigned. Apparently it's believed that Van Gogh disliked the painting and therefore didn't sign it for that reason. It took two years of chemical analysis, X-ray research and going through the letters of Vincent Van Gogh who wrote to his brother Theo describing the painting which is now deemed an authentic Van Gogh masterpiece. Its current value borders on priceless.

So doing a 'house sweep' perhaps with a person who knows something about antiques could be a great investment in your time in order to potentially discover hidden wealth that you are currently totally unaware of. The chances of making money through unearthing some sort of find is 1000 times greater than buying 100 lottery tickets.

7: Subscriptions, Rentals, Licensing and Royalties

Of all the people in the world who create money from their activities, few think like an entrepreneur and most opt for fully paid work. They in effect sell their time for cash. Nothing wrong with this, though ultimately at some point in one's life the body is likely to say, "that's enough". The solution is to be paid many times for one piece of work rather than paid for each piece of work. Artistes who emerged in the twentieth century in the world of film, image design, television and music soon realised great riches from recording their song, lyrics, image or story then agreeing royalty payments thereafter. Well-known artists like Paul McCartney and Elton John were amongst the earliest 'big hitters' and still derive millions of pounds each year from original studio recordings. And you don't need to be a McCartney or John to have a slice of this means of money creation.

Yes you can create stories and music and sell it with a royalty agreement in place, but you could also consider other ways of deriving on-going income.

Today young people turn to opportunities like YouTube to make regular money as vloggers or video loggers. Successful YouTube channels can be fully-fledged full time businesses creating equally exciting full time incomes however there is still the need to 'keep doing it' in order for the money to keep rolling in and the subscriber list high, usually in excess of 100,000 to start making any kind of money.

The other option is a website providing a service where one piece of work can be paid for many times over by the subscribers who support the site. This has not been as successful recently as it used to be twenty to thirty years ago. This is down to the fact that the younger mind is less open to ongoing payments however small the sums involved.

What does bring in wealth is licensing an idea, process or use of a product all done on-line. Training companies for example can create a training course and then license other trainers to use it.

A car valeting firm has created a 'perfect' way of cleaning a car and even created specialist equipment. The company then licenses others to use their process paying them monthly royalties in exchange. Is there something you are good at that you could make a template or model for, then sell the use of your innovation to others building a regular monthly income? If you think about this, it is in effect creating a pension payment each month based on no pension fund. The pension could even commence whilst still in your 20s. Author Timothy Ferris has much more detail to offer in his best seller *The Four Hour Work Week* which is all about giving up your day job or at the very least finding ways to be able to spend more time doing what you want versus having to do what you need to in order to pay the rent or mortgage.

Probably licensing is safer than franchising because there are less legal implications and liability involved, though you should draft in the help of a legal eagle to be clear and sure of how to do either.

A well-known British TV comedian created a website and used to record skits in his kitchen then upload it for fans in their millions. It was initially free until he tried an experiment of charging something like a pound a month to see if people still subscribed. They did! He made millions each month, but then went back to offering it for free as he didn't need the money!

There's also much to be said for creating 'an app' either via Apple (iOS) or Android or both. Having an in-built subscription with the right app can sky rocket you to mega success very fast and surprisingly many lacklustre apps still make good money simply because they are the only app in existence that does a particular service or task.

8: Open a 'Never-Never' Account

In days gone by this term referred to hire purchase. Here it means something different. Think about opening a separate bank or investment account where you are only in credit and never debit. In fact, imagine putting money into the account but never opening a single statement. This means that over time you would have absolutely no idea how much is in the account and all that you'd be doing is accumulating cash.

So what's the point of doing this? Well, apart from creating a growing asset which is always a good idea, you also have a nest egg that might make a massive difference to you one day. Like spending, saving small amounts of cash sporadically mounts up particularly if you don't check how much it's amounting to. You will be staggered by the sum you save over a few years. Meanwhile the game here is not to check the balance. Have a few standing orders going in and also make ad hoc credits. Yet never-never check the balance and…

- pay in money regularly
- never make a withdrawal

I've had a number of clients over the years refer to their investment accounts as "the money I give to Dean". It's a mindset thing helping them to forget the money for a future date and by feeling like they've handed it over to me to look after it for them they don't have access to it (even if they do).

9: Insure Yourself and Become Wealthy Overnight.

Buying life insurance and/or income protection is one of those things that we put off or simply prefer not to think about, yet from the wealth perspective you can buy yourself an impressive estate for a relatively small amount of money each month. Naturally the younger you are, the better the deal. Today many Life insurance companies will allow you to make a claim for a serious illness and/or a terminal condition.

People who neglect this aspect of their finances always regret the lack of foresight when the worst does happen around their health and life expectancy. If you are young enough and healthy enough you could acquire a seven-figure estate in a matter of a few weeks as well as low monthly payment.

There's the old story called 'The Money Machine'. Imagine that you have in your lounge the mechanical device which churns out fresh banknotes on the basis of £200 a day. The notes produced are legal currency and may be spent anywhere in the world with no tax implications. The question to you is, "How much would you insure this machine for?" Think about this…over time it would produce hundreds of thousands if not millions of pounds. Yet you can't guard it and therefore it could easily be stolen or destroyed. What value would you place on this item that produces legitimate cash every working day?

The likelihood is you would insure this machine for a lot of money, so why do we not insure ourselves in similar vein? We are all 'money machines' that cannot be guarded after all. The more you think about this, the more you realise the need and wisdom of protecting yourself through insurance.

10: Create a Social Group

If you were to connect with like-minded people, there is a good chance of collectively coming up with some great ideas. Yes this can be done on applications like Facebook, yet equally it would work well on a face-to-face basis. Like minds attract, and like minds can motivate and inspire each other. That's why *Weight Watchers* is so successful. Consider a Money Ideas group or Entrepreneurs' Club.

This chapter is also about *Time* versus *Money* versus *Your intention*. Going from rags to riches in a very short time frame is more common than you might imagine. The biggest barrier to success is yourself and it's getting control of that little voice in your head that tells you that you can't and there's no time left.

At the time of writing this book I have seen a television programme about life at 100. More people than ever before are living into three figures. More people in their 90s are finding paid employment, some to supplement their incomes but many more want something interesting to do where they can still feel valued. People in their 80s are still working in theatre and the arts, many still do punishing schedules in movies and TV series. Vast sums of people in their 70s have forgotten their ages and simply say 70 is the new 50. And people in their 60s are deciding that it's time for a second career or a new business venture because retirement is not for them.

If you are not in any of the above, you are 59 or younger and still have time to create a better financial future. Of course you can retire, spend lots of time doing all manner of things and have a ball. Great. As long as you know you have a choice and age is and always will be a number to those with a positive mindset.

Character Notes and Steps

WHAT ARE THE MOST IMPORTANT MESSAGES?

ACTION IDEAS

ACTION STEPS – *MY COMMITMENT*

4

Money Paradigms

"You are free to create your own paradigms instead of simply accepting those presented to you by others."
Russell Eric Dobda

A paradigm is a set view or belief which for some people is unchangeable. Here is the dictionary definition:

"Intellectual perception or view, accepted by an individual or a society as a clear example, model or pattern of how things work in the world".

Where money is concerned, we are all governed whether we like it or not, by certain paradigms. These 'set beliefs' are often handed down by our parents or learned in school from teachers or other children and not only do they shape our beliefs about money but ultimately our bank account balances and overall wealth.

You will probably remember other children in your class at school and how they used to operate around money which was different to you. Some would have liked to save, others to spend, and in-betweeners who probably accounted for the large majority. There are invariably a few very canny children who have had some parental 'programming' about money with an intelligence about how to use it and even make more of it.

Here are Seven Money Paradigms. Each one either currently affects your thoughts and beliefs around money, or has had some historic influence on you.

If you were to interview exceptional money users who are normally self made millionaires in their own right, you will notice that their beliefs in these six areas rejects the thinking of the vast majority of the population.

Take each of the 4 areas in turn and give yourself a score out of 10. The top score of 10 indicates you accept the belief. Scoring lower or 0 means you reject the belief. In theory the lower your score, the richer you probably are. And here's the magic wand part. If you can get your thinking to a much lower score, you are likely to start to grow your wealth considerably!

FIRST PARADIGM: I'LL NEVER MAKE THE RICH LIST

The Paradigm: *Getting on the Rich List is something one could never aspire to attain unless you are already quite rich, partly famous, a Lottery winner or you've managed to come into some unusually good fortune by accident or extraordinary co-incidence.*

Victoria Wood of *The Telegraph* reported that a fortune in excess of £100m is now required to be in the top 1000 of the richest people in the United Kingdom. She went on to say that, "the combined wealth of the 1,000 richest men and women in Britain has more than doubled in the last ten years, according to the *Sunday Times* Rich List. The wealthiest 1,000 individuals and families now have a combined fortune of £547.126 billion, up from £249.615 billion in 2005, despite the world economy being gripped by a punishing recession over much of the last decade.

'Plain old millionaires' increasingly struggle to count themselves among the mega-rich, with a fortune in excess of £100 million. That is £15 million higher than previous, while in 1997 it took a personal wealth of 'just' £15 million to make the grade. The list includes 117 billionaires, up from 104 last year. They account for a total wealth of £325.131 billion and 80 of them are based in London.

It means the capital has more sterling billionaires than any other city in the world. London-based Ukrainian businessman Len Blavatnik whose empire includes the Warner Music Group, is named the wealthiest man, with an estimated fortune of £13.17 billion. He jumped from fourth last year after seeing his wealth rise by more than £3 billion, according to the list. Mr Blavatnik took over top spot from brothers Sri and Gopi Hinduja, who were nudged into second despite their fortune rising by £1.1 billion to £13 billion.

Galen and George Weston and family, who run a retail empire including Selfridges and Primark, enjoyed a particularly prosperous year, with their wealth soaring by £3.7 billion to £11 billion. New entries include George and Amal Clooney, the recently married actor and lawyer, who have a combined wealth of £121 million. But not all those in the top 25 have seen their bank balances bulge. And new money flooding into Britain from abroad is said to have pushed many Britons down the list. Of Britain's 117 billionaires, only 62 are British.

As an example of how old money is suffering, the Queen has dropped out of the wealthiest top 300 for the first time, despite increasing her personal wealth by £10 million this year to £340 million. The list charts wealth including land, property, assets or significant shares but excludes bank accounts. Steel magnate Lakshmi Mittal and Chelsea Football Club chairman Roman Abramovich saw their fortunes fall by £1.05 billion and £1.23 billion respectively, the list claimed. Sir Paul McCartney topped the list of 40 musical millionaires. With a personal fortune of £730 million, the former Beatle is well ahead of his nearest rival Andrew Lloyd Webber, who is worth an estimated £650 million in comparison.

Adele, who is estimated to be worth £50 million, was named richest young musician in the UK and Ireland. Second place in the chart, made up of acts aged 30 or under, goes to the four members of One Direction and former bandmate Zayn Malik who are said to be worth "£25 million each".

In the top 20, 'poor Richard Branson' manages to scrape in at number 20 with just over £4.1b give or take £100m.

Having got all of that in your head, there is no wonder that most people completely separate such wealth from themselves, but this paradigm is not about wanting to be in the list, it's making a much bigger assumption that money goes to money and that if you haven't got much already, there's no point even thinking about getting vast amounts in your life time.

The key here is to be able to think around the success of an individual and be more interested in their story and route to the big time. By studying wealthy people's stories you will be able to see readily identifiable patterns that anyone can follow. How much you then make as a result would be decided on how ambitious you are. I personally would say it is less about ambition and more about need. Need over Greed. There is always a point at which your brain kicks in and tells you - spend any more time making money and you won't live long enough to enjoy any of it. Despite this there are many 'Scrooges' who live in the world 'enjoying' poverty while there is untold wealth under the bed.

Second Paradigm: Expect and be Disappointed

The Paradigm: *There is little point expecting the door bell to ring with news of a large amount of money coming your way because in reality this just never happens. Expecting money is simply leading yourself to greater disappointment.*

It's interesting to note how people give up on creating a wealthy life very early on. If you don't expect something it's likely to never happen. Expectation creates a mindset that seems to search for the very thing you have yet to discover to achieve what you desire.

This is the subject of the best selling book and DVD *The Secret* by Rhonda Byrne. Wikipedia describes it as, "a best-selling 2006 self help book based on the film of the same name. It's about the Law of Attraction and claims that the right kind of positive mindset can create life-changing results such as increased happiness, health, and wealth.

The book has sold more than 21 million copies worldwide and has been translated into 46 languages. Influenced by Wallace Wattles' 1910 book *The Science of Getting Rich* which Byrne received from her daughter during a time of personal trauma, she went on to create her own interpretation while reading and synthesizing several classic books of modern-day teachers who spoke about ancient money attraction wisdom.

The book includes many quotes from these people. After being featured in two episodes of *The Oprah Winfrey Show*, the book reached the top of the *New York Times's* bestseller list, where it remained for 146 consecutive weeks. The essence of this book, which is better ingested as a movie, is that creating an expectation about something will cause it to eventually happen. The more powerful the mental imagery and expectation, the more likely that the end goal will materialise.

If you think about this quite logically, we are probably what we continually think about. If your expectation is to leave school and join the family bakery business, then that's highly likely where you'll end up for your entire working life. Equally if you see yourself as an entrepreneur you may join the family business, but soon find yourself re-shaping the enterprise, franchising the brand and growing the opportunity exponentially.

My own take on *The Secret* is that it's a good starting point to make your mind more open to possibility. So how do you make monetary expectation a daily habit?

1 - Decide on what you want and why you want it.

2 - Think about how you could achieve your goal.

3 - Investigate ways of achievement through research.

4 - Consider creating a scrapbook of images that support your desire.

5 - Keep imagining you have your desire already.

Though these five steps may appear obvious and even too easy to make any difference and work, both sports and life coaches who have psychology backgrounds endorse the theory and practice of this mindset because it has proven to work, especially in sports.

The part of your brain that helps expectation is called the 'RAS' or Reticular Activation System. Though its function isn't solely about awareness, it is responsible for helping you to focus on things at a high intensity level. This in turn stimulates subconscious thinking, and whenever you engage the subconscious you are most likely to get extra mental activity on things that are important to you. That's why sitting in a bath or driving a car can create breakthrough thoughts because by getting into a relaxed state this is the first trigger to more open thought allowing your subconscious to switch its creative mode on.

Imagine watching a top tennis star dominate Wimbledon. He or she is weary, highly stressed and yet mentally tough when it matters most. In creating wealth and well being, mental toughness matters. It's probably when you least feel like expecting the best to happen that you most need to keep thinking the thoughts and living out the desired outcomes in your head. This also separates the serious contenders from the wish-mores who give up at the first feeling of difficulty.

Whether you are an Andy Murray or Tom Daley, sports psychology plays a critical role of any peak performer's training programme which is very much about unequivocally expecting huge slices of success from yourself. Sports Coaching guru Phil Jackson said, "Wisdom is always an overmatch for strength. People in the Hall of Fame and Olympic champions, backed by decades of empirical research, all agree that the proper use of psychology strategies can significantly improve any athlete's performance".

So what is the correlation between sports psychology and money creation psychology?

- Super confidence in your abilities. (Expectation).
- The ability to focus when distracted. (RAS).
- High motivation at all times. (Mental Imagery).
- Dominion over anxiety, frustration, and discouragement.
- Clear-cut short, medium and long term goals.
- Visualisation on a daily basis of what you want.
- Positive language promoting positive thinking.
- Upbeat body language to get that feeling of success.

THIRD PARADIGM: DISCLOSURE MEANS NO SECRETS

The Paradigm: *The majority of very rich people are often well known to us. It's quite a challenge to hide wealth in the form of large houses, fast sports cars, expensive accoutrements such as Omega watches, Cartier jewellery, designer clothes and even an entourage of helpers and minders. Therefore, it's easier perhaps for people to flaunt their fortunes. We hear of the 'sympathy billionaires' who cry out about their difficult lives, having to be careful where they go, who they connect with and being ultra cautious of the possibility of being kidnapped. But could the seed of this paradigm lie in the simple concept called ego?*

Today however, the sudden mega rich like Lottery winners seem to be getting wiser. Fewer multi-million-pound lottery winners broadcast their good fortune to the world compared with the past. Previously many lotto winners have found that going public was not only the worst thing they could do, but massively contributed to their downfall. This included the permanent loss of family connections and life long friends. It's also quite shocking how many solvent people win the lottery and then soon go bankrupt after a massive win.

Callie Rogers from Workington in Cumbria won £1.9m in 2003 when she was just 16 years old. She wasted her winnings buying things like a fancy car and employing her boyfriend to be the chauffeur. Also £200,000 on holidays and £450,000 on clothes.

When she discovered her boyfriend was more interested in the cash than her, she tried to commit suicide but survived. Christopher Donnelly, another winner of the same age, was successful in his suicide attempt after not being able to cope with the publicity.

The National Endowment for Financial Education did some research on Lottery winners estimating that a massive 70% of people who suddenly receive a large sum of money will lose all of it within a few short years.

For example, Jack Whittaker who was already a millionaire won $315 million in West Virginia, USA. Just four years later he declared that he was practically penniless. Apparently Whittaker gave away millions of dollars, but people also stole hundreds of thousands from him. He also lost a granddaughter in a drug overdose during the same period.

Most ordinary people who come into large sums of money become victims of their own lack of financial savvy it's said. People also come under great pressure from friends, relatives and a host of others wanting their cash.

So when is disclosing your wealth a good idea? Or should having money be your best kept secret? Research and case histories suggest that telling the world, even close friends and family is ill advised, and months of thought and reflection should go by before deciding on whether revealing one's new found fortune is the right thing to do.

This is fine where the Lottery is concerned, but I am going to suggest 'Disclosure' also relates to many in general for the very same reasons. Whether you like it or not you will be judged on figures which are best never discussed.

Telling others (other than your partner) how much you make, how much money you have and other financial information creates two potential negative reactions.

1 - Your subconscious will notice the reaction of the person you share this delicate information with. If their reaction is veiled in negativity or jealousy it may inadvertently program your mind going forward.

2 - Self sabotage may occur when you discuss things that are deemed by the brain as highly volatile and changeable. For example, have you ever said you were going to get something good and then it never happened? Or have you explained to someone that you may get promoted and after telling six people it was finally confirmed that you didn't get the new position? Talking about money for no good reason can have the same effect. Also declaring you are going well financially may trigger your subconscious to slow things down because it's not in keeping with deeper beliefs and paradigms about yourself.

Best avoid 'Disclosure' on money matters unless there is a very good reason for it. And if you choose to disclose make sure it is with people you can confidently confide in.

Fourth Paradigm: Rapid Loss is very Real

The Paradigm: *It suggests that it's far easier to lose everything in one go, than to make an overnight fortune.* Let's look at some examples of it.

Rapid Loss Example: MC Hammer.
Musician success MC Hammer was worth $30m initially, but soon started to spend wildly on cars, real estate and the good life. In record time after poor decision making he was bankrupt and never ever recovered. On his day in court, many of the people he had helped and given money to were absent at his own time of need.

Rapid Loss Example: Sean Quinn
Successful Irish business man Sean Quinn was the richest man in Ireland in 2008 with a net worth of £6b. Sadly he lost it all on one single bad decision after investing significantly with Anglo Irish Bank, then borrowing funds from his insurance company. The Recession took its toll and he could not recover from the ensuing debt.

Rapid Loss Example: Denise and Chris Tudor Whelan

This British couple had assets of £35m with an income stream of £20,000 a month. They owned a six bedroomed house worth nearly £1m and sent their children to private schools. Money was never a problem. But after the banking collapse they became jobseekers on an allowance of £217 a fortnight. They hit rock-bottom with a food budget of just £5 a day. So what was their poor decision if there was one? "We put all our eggs in one basket and lost everything".

So Rapid Loss does happen. What about the opposite happening? Overnight Success?

British man Ashley Revell sold everything he had and took the equivalent of $135,300 to the USA to bet his entire net worth on the spin of a roulette wheel. There was less than a 50-50 chance of winning. A 47.3% chance in fact on the American roulette table. Within seconds of placing his bet on RED, he had doubled his money with $270,600 at his elbow. Then he left the casino resisting the invitation to have one more spin.

There are of course many examples of building wealth at speed, and the point is that money can be made or lost very quickly. The paradigm of it not being possible to do anything positive overnight is certainly not true. However, the number of people losing it all overnight is dwarfed by those who make the big time as fast. It's just that, sadly, the media prefers reporting on losers rather than winners.

Where it may be unlikely for you to go from rags to riches in 24 hours, this is much more feasible than the opposite.

By accepting this as a real possibility, the mind can be opened to exciting possibilities of smaller surprising 'wins' happening more frequently which all eventually equate to a rather rapid accumulation of success.

Fifth Paradigm: Investment is for the Rich

The Paradigm: *When you think investment you really need to have a tidy sum put by as this is the only way to do it.*

In 1983 at the age of 21 a young woman invests £100 a month into a private pension. Each year she increases the sum to match inflation. The government are also adding 25% to the pot for her and the fund she invests in rises sharply over a time period. With the addition of lump sums occasionally invested she has more than £1m on her 60th birthday to retire on.

Such is the power of compound interest on good investment returns. Curiously, many other young people in their 20s who had the same opportunity decided to pass on it because:

a) they felt they were far too young or

b) they didn't want to tie themselves down to a regular 'payment', even though they would be paying themselves.

In the same year a man buys a one bedroomed flat just off Park Lane in Mayfair for £120,000. There is a glut of houses and flats in London. There are also studio apartments a stone's throw from Baker Street W1 for just £40,000 that no one wants to buy. The man gets his pied-à-terre valued in 2014. It's now worth a few pounds north of £4m.

In these two examples it could be argued at the time that there was nothing particularly unusual in these straight forward relatively safe investments. However, why didn't others do the same? It was less about not wanting to invest, more about the notion that investment is for people with lots of money. This of course is not true. There are many things you can explore investing in which include buying shares in a business. The success factor in investments is often about time. But isn't this just another name for saving?

Saving is putting money away when you have it. Strict saving is putting a set amount of money away each month regardless. Dynamic saving is strict saving plus having the determination to add additional amounts to the pot whenever circumstances allow and investment is doing all of it plus looking for higher returns in such things as a property or attractive pension scheme. If in doubt, save. If you dare, invest. The latter can bring more exciting times too.

Sixth Paradigm: No Financial Leverage

The Paradigm: *Financial Leverage is for smart people who are probably already rich.*

You've probably heard of the expression 'Cash is King'. This is a form of leverage that can put you in a strong position. Leverage is not about leaning on people with less money than you, it's about having more money at your disposal that allows you to negotiate better for example.

You should also bear in mind that even without money, if you are going to make a purchase and have the means to complete the transaction, then the other well-known adage is 'The Customer is King'.

In the UK especially, Brits seem very reluctant to negotiate. It seems not the done thing. Yet Leverage through having the upper hand will help you make more money and allow you to accumulate more wealth if only you were prepared to do it. It requires:

- awareness of an opportunity to negotiate
- a desire to keep more of your money in the transaction
- a boldness to speak up for yourself
- a knowledge that people respect people who apply leverage

It might also be a good idea to read a basic negotiation skills book for good measure and there are some negotiation tips coming up.

The Paradigm: *One of the most potent anti-catalysts for wealth is the belief in Lack, also known as scarcity. If you see the word scarcity it may make you automatically think of homeless people sitting on the streets of major cities begging for cash for example. Or it may trigger a deep- seated belief that money is scarce and not everyone can have it in a large quantity. Where sympathy is due, the sympathy should be for the paradigm as opposed to the reality of money scarcity which I suggest is a false belief.*

In the west, the majority of people living on the streets are normally relatively healthy individuals unlike the east in poverty environments where the poor may also be disabled or physically impaired that prevents them from working. Third world countries that have no social security systems and live impoverished lives with no choice sometimes have to beg... but they too have probably bought into the belief that lack of money is a stark reality in life.

There is no lack of money. Governments may talk about the scarcity of money, but they also have the power to conjure it up from thin air by printing more when needed, cleverly attributed to a technical term called *Quantitative Easing*. Perhaps then we should be much more aware of *Abundance Factors.*

Factor 1: Creativity

Factor 2: Ingenuity

Factor 3: Exploration

Factor 4: Collaboration

Factor 5: Entrepreneurship

Factor 6: Latent Potential

CREATIVITY

When people are creative, either by themselves or by inspiring others and working with them, the output released is potentially of greater value than working with traditional ideas.

INGENUITY

Slightly different to Creativity, Ingenuity is often looking at something that already exists then re-examining it from a different standpoint. This could also be about turning something on its head to bring it to life in a new and refreshing way.

EXPLORATION

Exploration is delving into what you already have. Often we forget assets and ideas that have been hanging around for years, and only by checking out our resources do we make discoveries about things we have forgotten about. This can also relate to skills and abilities.

COLLABORATION

There are a growing number of networking groups in businesses today. Working in collaboration is a great way to expand thinking, connections and working relationships. It can also be an idea to thoroughly trawl your contacts list, remind yourself who you know and then reconnect. The old adage, "it's not what you know, but who you know" is still alive and well today and entirely relevant.

ENTREPRENEURSHIP

This rather grand term hides a simple concept. The passion for an idea, self motivation and a desire to create wealth through providing a host of genuine benefits to others; something that attracts great rewards. Yes there can be challenges, but an entrepreneur who is prepared to think things through and get advice from others is an exciting prospect to him or herself as well as the world at large.

LATENT POTENTIAL

We are often told that we have skills and abilities that we're not using, and this is most certainly true. When anyone is taught something and goes on to use the skill, the skill itself must have always been there; it was the 'how' that was missing in the teaching. To release latent potential, boldness is the first step.

In the Channel 4 TV show *Faking It* people were taken into professions that were entirely alien to them, then coached over 30 days to be able to pass themselves off in this industry or profession. A student became a bouncer, a burger van owner became a cordon bleu chef (and won a competition), and a painter and decorator went from £20 an hour to £2,000 a painting as an impressionist artist.

The inference here is that when we say we lack resources, we are actually forgetting the things that are not scarce. Things we all have at our fingertips.

The next time you are thinking of giving money to a person begging in the street, perhaps five minutes of your time to share ways they could improve their lives could be infinitely more valuable to them than a few pound coins. However, they will probably be blocked by their own powerful paradigms and see cash as the only solution and life changing ideas as totally unhelpful. When you see such people, they can actually help you. Because what you are looking at is an extraordinary good example of what paradigms do to the human spirit which is no longer free. They are imprisoned by paradigms and false dilemmas which is sad to see, yet a great visual reminder for you.

Now because there are so many paradigms out there, I want to separate them out a little by looking separately at *Money Myths*. As you will soon discover, there is a subtle difference between a paradigm and a myth.

Character Notes and Steps

WHAT ARE THE MOST IMPORTANT MESSAGES?

ACTION IDEAS

ACTION STEPS – *MY COMMITMENT*

5

Money Myths that Haunt Us

"Myths are a waste of time. They prevent progression..."
Barbara Streisand

A Myth is defined as a traditional or legendary story, usually concerning a being or hero or event, with or without a determinable basis of fact or a natural explanation, especially one that is concerned with deities or demigods and explains some practice, rite, or phenomenon of nature. Unlike a paradigm, a myth is openly discussed and has little to do with subconscious programming.

For example the historical characters of Robin Hood and King Arthur are shrouded in mythology. No one absolutely knows for sure if these people were real or not. I remember when I was young we visited the Robin Hood Centre in Nottingham and during the course of the visit had to ultimately decide whether our hero was a 'myth' and join the evil (at least to my young mind) Sherriff's men or 'legend' and be branded an Outlaw. I took the obvious route and proudly accepted the staff member's stamp of approval having the word 'Outlaw' stamped in green ink on the back of my hand. Imagine my surprise when I turned and saw my father had taken the 'myth' route and joined the Sherriff of Nottingham, becoming a gentleman of the town!

Other myths include William Shakespeare and whether he actually wrote all his plays and whether or not there is a Loch Ness Monster.

Today, we are plagued with myths about money that are constantly propagated by idle chit-chat, television stories, especially the soap opera genre, and self-fulfilling prophesies often based on wanting, lack and poor self esteem.

A major myth that is changing in recent times is about young people and success. In the last 20 to 30 years some youngsters in their teens and as young as 12 have set up successful corporations and made their first million before leaving school.

I would like to cover several myths together:

- The young can't make serious money
- You have to have a unique idea to make it big
- Real opportunities are few and far between today.
- Everything big has already been done.

Money Myths Around Young People

Youth, passion rather than innovation and abundant opportunities are all around... Some children can make lots of cash at a very early age, the majority do not however due to parental control and the acceptance of myths around youth and money.

Money From Flip-Flops

Let's take a product that many would have turned their nose up at. Rather like Starbucks selling and re-branding coffee in 1971, so it was with flip-flop shoes in recent times.

A 15-year-old girl recently became a millionaire by selling flip-flops. Madison Robinson is the name of this once spotty teen from Galveston Island, Texas who began her flip-flop business at the tender age of just 13. In fact, she was only 8 when she dreamed up the simple idea to sell flip-flops decorated with fish. The foot wear is manufactured without punch-out holes in the soles so the straps don't pop out like they do in generic flip-flops. They also feature LED lights in the soles, making them popular with young beachgoers who are her target audience.

She didn't do it all on her own however, Madison had the complete support from her family that made a huge difference to her ultimate success. The venture is so profitable in fact that this teenager has already saved enough money to cover her college fees where she will study business acumen and related subjects to ensure she develops her entrepreneurialism to become even more successful when she leaves university. The *Daily Mail* newspaper, said that her products now sell online, in various retail outlets and at sixty *Nordstrom Stores* across America for around $20 a pair.

The flip-flops are also coming soon to a specialist website and Macy's store buyers in New York recently asked her to design a line just for women. More than 60,000 pairs sold in 2012, as a result making retail sales of at least $1.2 million.

It was reported on the internet that the 15-year-old draws all of her own designs and chooses colour combinations digitally. She has also learned how to pack shipments, stock the warehouse, explain her pricing, host a trade show booth and make a sales pitch. She gives away free 'Fish Flops' and volunteers for a charity that supports the children of fallen military heroes.

This has led to a major order from the Army's Post Exchange stores. At the Teen Choice Awards in 2011, she got celebrities to sign 300 pairs of Fish Flops for Texas Children's Hospital patients by donating 10,000 pairs of Fish Flops to a community shoe drive and supporting the Texas Parks & Wildlife's K-12 State Fish Art Contest.

British brothers Paul and Rob Forkan have done something similar in the UK with the same product, also at a young age - ignoring that other money myth about having competitors being an issue.

Here's what Rob said in his own words about his story of 'rags to riches'...

"My parents, Kevin and Sandra Forkan, were compassionate, fun loving and generous people who enjoyed travelling and wanted us to experience other cultures. In 2001, after selling their house in Croydon, they took us out of school and we headed for India, the place they loved most. The plan was to volunteer for humanitarian projects.

Despite the extreme hardship we witnessed we all loved India and its people. In 2004 we flew south to spend Christmas in Sri Lanka.

We stayed at the Neptune Hotel in Weligama, a small fishing village. After a fantastic Christmas Day on the beach, something happened on Boxing Day that would change our lives forever. Shortly after 8.30am, while we were still in our beds, the tsunami hit.

A 20-foot wave devastated our hotel. My younger brother Paul and I managed to survive by scrambling up onto the hotel roof. Tragically, my parents were swept away after getting my youngest brother Matty and sister Rosie to safety. I never saw them alive again. Dad was 54 and mum just 40.

Although we were battered, hungry, exhausted, barefoot and in shock, we managed to hitch lifts, travelling about 120 miles overland to the airport in Colombo. I returned to the UK and in the years that followed I combined travelling with various jobs. I worked as a lifeguard, later in customer service and then in advertising account management.

Paul also continued to travel and ended up in Australia, but we both retained a desire to help others, something we'd learned from our parents. Visiting India and other countries really does underline the fact that many people are much worse off than you are. After a heavy night at a music festival I woke up with a dreadful hangover. I remember saying I had a 'mouth like Gandhi's 'flip-flop'…

That was it my Eureka moment. Flip-flops! Having travelled around the world wearing them for years it was a product I knew well. I'd had other business ideas, but none I'd believed in as strongly.

And as well as a business idea, I had the basis for a brand name. We changed the spelling so as not to cause any offence. I rang Paul and he loved the idea. He returned to the UK and in 2011 we launched the business, 'Gandys' from my flat in Brixton. Our business idea was simple. We didn't try to reinvent the wheel, just to create a great product and a brand with a difference. One that donates some of its profits to helping desperately underprivileged children.

We haven't really outsourced anything. When starting up, some people might tell you that you shouldn't try to tackle this or that because you lack experience, but often you find that much of it is just common sense.

We've made mistakes, sure, but you learn from your experiences and move forward. When we told people we were launching a new flip-flop brand a few of them didn't think it was wise, but flip-flops have become hugely popular in the UK and, in any case, the plan was always to sell internationally. Global sales of flip-flops are huge, more than 220m pairs of Havanas are sold each year. We're new to the market, but there's more than enough room for us.

At the moment we're constantly being contacted by people all over the world who want to stock or buy our flip-flops and it's relentless. Soon we hope our products will be available in thirty countries. Many consumers are discerning and want to buy from brands that have a social conscience, but the product still has to be good.

The reaction to our flip-flops has been a bit crazy. We've had a lot of media attention and that's helped boost sales. You can buy our flip-flops from leading stockists such as Selfridges, House of Fraser, Sole Trader, Top Man, Schuh, Office, USC, FootAsylum and Asos.

People ask us what we're going to do once the first Gandy's orphanage is built and we tell them we're going to work harder so we can sell more flip-flops and build another one, then another, then another. We'll never stop."

3 Key Pieces of Advice

- Your products must be appealing. It's often the case that initial prototypes of products aren't as good as the final or current product now on sale. It's important to act on market research feedback to create a more attractive product.
- Go and speak to people who actually run their own businesses. You can pick up a lot of valuable advice by speaking to others.
- Even if you have a great product, interesting story and social enterprise dimension to what you're doing, you *must* be able to sell. If you can't sell, employ someone who can, otherwise your business won't succeed.

Money Heart - Gems of Wisdom

I particularly wanted to include stories about young people because us older ones buy into myths far more easily. It's not what you know as a child, it's your attitude and behaviours taught to you mainly by your parents. Those parents who have themselves got caught up in negative money myths from their parents and grandparents tend to pass these on to their offspring in complete ignorance. The top three 'Roots of Money Myths' are school lessons, the meal table at home and the games played as a child.

Money Heart is about passion, desire, obsession and wanting to make a difference. Younger minds tend to be more 'natural' with this approach. What is definitely in short supply are the people in general out there with a more feisty approach to money and its creation. The inner courage and fortitude to *go for it* rather than sit and wait for others to bring it to them. There is nothing wrong with gainful employment, but we can get stuck in the myth that considering self employment or setting up one's own sideline business is for a small group called 'entrepreneurs' and not for the masses. After all, isn't it easier to be part of the crowd and not have to think about where the next pay cheque is coming from?

For those that do consider a sideline business and love the idea and have no idea where to start, a good rule of thumb is to create something that solves a problem. The easier and bigger the problem solver, the more probable that you would be successful.

It's Difficult to Become Wealthy

If it were easy - everyone would be doing it. Wouldn't they?

Already mentioned is that most parents are quite (innocently) ignorant when it comes to programming their off spring about money, probably because they don't know enough themselves.

If you look at any young entrepreneur, you can track back to supportive parents, many of whom were young entrepreneurs themselves or had become inspired to become business aware early on. The brothers who set up Gandy's were inspired by parents who were adventurers rather than 9-5 types.

So the myth that it's difficult to become wealthy is the starting block for many and knowing how to side-step this mental barrier is the key to change.

The answer lies in changing habits and focusing on new values and beliefs. If you are someone who shares this mythical belief the good news is that you have already started to turn your ship around. The fact you are reading this book means you have an immense opportunity to create a new set of beliefs about wealth, money and a successful life regardless of the myths that continue to haunt everyone else.

Robert T Kiyosaki is the author of *Rich Dad Poor Dad: What the rich teach their children that others do not!* He has written a host of money books including some with known billionaires.

Going back in time, two classics are *The Magic of Thinking Big* by David J Schwartz and further back still to the all time classic, Napoleon Hill's *Think and Grow Rich*. There are many such books that you could read if you are entrenched in old money myths. Let's remind you of another one.

To Make Money you must Work Hard

This is an interesting myth because it has a lot of truth in it even though it's not ultimately the case.

There are so many successful entrepreneurs who are interviewed and say, "The secret of my success is hard work". Yet hard work itself cannot possibly make you wealthy, otherwise the majority of the world's population would become wealthy overnight simply selecting the hardest work to get involved in. Hard work can contribute to success but is absolutely not the main factor. Most people *have to work hard* to get paid relatively small sums the world over and few ever hit the big time.

Businessman Sergi Trivino once said, "Hard work without a purpose is like a Ferrari without a steering wheel". When people see a successful individual they automatically equate the image with a hard worker and miss all the other clues to their achievement. It's also true to say that people who adore and love what they do forget they are working hard because it doesn't feel that way.

There is nothing wrong with hard work, and often hard work is critical for success. The point really is believing that hard work in itself is all you need to do to become super wealthy, and this has no foundation in truth.

You can lose Friends if you Become Wealthy Suddenly

Which is why you should not disclose money matters. There was the UK lottery winner who was so pleased with his £6m win he decided to buy four of his closest friends new houses all nearby so they could stay in touch and continue to be friends. Within a year they had all sold their new homes and moved away having nothing more to do with their generous friend.

The Rags to Riches Idea is Pure Hollywood

It's probably true to say that those going from rags to riches has in fact increased in the past fifty years and the signs are that this number will keep growing especially with technology making it easier for everyone with a good idea to have a stake in S.W.S. or Sudden Wealth Syndrome. This has been seen recently in the 'app' marketplace.

Richard Branson started the virgin group with just £300. He kicked off his career by creating a magazine at 16 in early 1970 and founded a mail order record company.

Deborah Meadon created a multi-million pound family leisure business from scratch and is now worth £40m and she is well known for her appearances on Dragon's Den.

Charles Dunstone who is worth £1.49b started the Carphone Warehouse with £6,000 selling mobile phones from his flat.

John Hunt began his property career with £100 that he borrowed to buy a one bedroom converted flat for £4500. Then in 1981 at 28 he founded Foxton's estate agents with a school friend.

Money Never brings Happiness

No it doesn't - not if you don't want it to. Such is the **inter-fear-ence** in our minds that we convince ourselves of things that just aren't true. Of course money can bring happiness and only with the wrong decision making and mindset will it bring the reverse which is the same for anything. This also applies to other things like friendships, where you decide to live, who you choose as your partner and even the weather. The linked myth is that Money will always make you happier. If all else fails, be rich and choose to be unhappy in comfort.

Money is the Root of All Evil

As most people are aware, money has never been reported as the root of all evil but as the Bible says it's the love of money that can be. Money itself is a tool, and like electricity, it can help or harm us if used in the wrong way.

It's also quite in order to strive to create a better life for oneself and one's family, indeed for others around you who are not so fortunate or positive minded. It's inevitably the greed element that perhaps is likely to skew one's relationship and experience of making money, enjoying what it can bring, and the keeping hold of it.

Paradigm & Myth Deletion Board

The way to dispel myths and re-program mental paradigms, not just for you but other members of your family is the creation of a PHOTO WALL. This idea has been extensively used by schools, businesses, communities and yes, entrepreneurs. It's an expose of your dreams and with a photo wall in a place that others can access, it can be a collaboration.

Character Notes and Steps

WHAT ARE THE MOST IMPORTANT MESSAGES?

ACTION IDEAS

ACTION STEPS – *MY COMMITMENT*

Part Two

MONEY HEAD

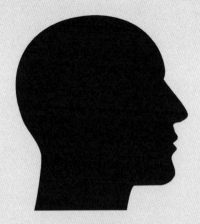

Business as an idea. Money Streams. Additional Income Flow.
More Classical Ideas & Concepts.

6

Is Entrepreneurship the Answer?

"The true entrepreneur is a doer, not a dreamer."
Nolan Bushnell, entrepreneur.

What do Anita Roddick, Duncan Banatyne and Bill Gates have in common apart from having made money within successful businesses?

It's often said that we either have the 'DNA' in our genes to create money or we don't and that most people simply don't have what it takes.

This can be a dangerous limiting belief; one that creates the barrier to success for the majority of those wanting to improve their lives, especially via business success. Is business acumen also linked to this? In other words, the knowledge and know-how to make good money decisions? There is one over-arching word for all this... *entrepreneurship*. Whereas the idea of being an entrepreneur is not necessarily something that most people are drawn to, it's something that anyone can become through personal choice.

Many entrepreneurs will say that they stumbled into it early on in their life. Maybe something was triggered in their minds from something they experienced or saw. Today entrepreneurs have been known to start from the age of 4. Equally, there are some who only decide to become entrepreneurs after they have retired or after a successful career. But is becoming an entrepreneur even necessary? Let's assume for a moment that it could be a 'Money-Head' opportunity to acquire more wealth and well-being.

Probably the challenge with entrepreneurship is the title!

THE 4 ENTREPRENEUR TYPES

TYPE 1: THE NATURAL

The natural entrepreneur is probably the type we are all aware of. This individual carries the flag for entrepreneurship and comes across as somebody with special skills, innate abilities, risk-based thinking and a flare for business.

In the TV show 'Dragon's Den' syndicated across the world, you have a lair of typical natural entrepreneurs. They come across as confident individuals who are intelligent but also perhaps judgmental at the same time with strong opinions.

Of course this has much to do with the type of show it is, yet it's fair to say that this representation matches the general perception for the natural entrepreneur. Their business psyche is very much about turning one unit of money into hundreds or thousands if possible in a relatively short timeframe. This means their effort is rewarded and recognised.

The biggest problem with the natural entrepreneur is that it does very little to encourage people on the sideline who would like to roll their sleeves up in a start-up opportunity. Instead the sideliner goes through much self-doubt and limiting beliefs based on their perception of somebody who appears beyond ordinary. And though we all love to see somebody who is self-made, the majority of us still disassociate ourselves from it at the same time. It's the same as talent shows on television where judges are seen to be naturals as singers or record producers. Any contestant is going to have a hard time not allowing this aspect to deflect their ability to do a good performance.

Finally, as a 'natural' it's most unlikely this applies to you as you would not be reading this book in the first place. You would have gone out and done it by now and be counting the money in your bank account.

Type 2: The Deep-Ender

Imagine this, you suddenly come across a great idea. Something that you are sure will make you a small fortune. The adrenaline is rushing and you can't wait to get started. Raising a little cash you engage in your project or new business. Within a couple of days you are really going for it and then it occurs to you that you're an entrepreneur in the making. You've jumped in with both feet however you have your fingers crossed behind your back!

There are many 'Deep-Ender' entrepreneurs in the world. Some have succeeded but most have crashed and burned. It's like catching a bug it takes over your whole being, making you make snap decisions - not all of them good ones. Deep–Enders are notoriously bad at figures and have no idea about profit and loss, cash flow and turnover. Basically they assume that their product will be so good, they will make all the money they need and at the same time everything will work out financially.

Are there any known successful Deep-Ender entrepreneurs? Mark Zuckerberg is probably one such example. His attention to detail through professional advisors makes a big difference in turning a good idea into a mega one. However, on the whole, jumping into the deep end and hoping everything will work out should be avoided.

The only positive thing to be said for Deep–Enders, is that it is fast track to learning how not to be an entrepreneur. Many successful people found themselves jumping in the deep end, making a complete mess of things, then going into 'Phoenix Mode', rising from the ashes and making business number two a big success.

If you are currently in a deep-ender situation or are a potential Deep- Ender entrepreneur, then look at type 4 as an alternative approach.

<u>TYPE 3: THE RELUCTANT</u>

Anyone who is not in group 1, 2 or 4 will automatically be a 'Reluctant' which is just about everyone else in the world. There's no doubt that everyone who hasn't gone forward as an entrepreneur has a reluctant streak inside of them that they simply do not want to act upon. The idea of this is quite exciting when you think about it.

It means we can all do it and that entrepreneurship is simply a latent ability that we need to tap into. If when you started to read this chapter you were already disassociating yourself from being entrepreneurial, the good news is that you are a Reluctant and that you can do something about it. The solution lies in type 4, and a key factor for going forward is *desire*. You need to really want to break free from your reluctance and achieve a new mindset that will take you where you want to go.

<u>TYPE 4: THE STRATEGIST</u>

This type of entrepreneur is probably the smartest because there are no assumptions. It starts with choosing to become a 'Strategist' and knowing to a large extent how it can be achieved.

The qualities of a Strategist starts with knowing your personal current limitations/ gaps that need addressing. Knowing what you don't know and knowing where to look for answers. In addition, being prepared to travel slower than you'd like to, ultimately ensuring that you get it right at the same time. A Strategist is also happy to plan first then take appropriate action. They want results not simply to look good in front of others. (Some Naturals want to keep being an entrepreneur long after they've made all the money they could ever spend).

Finally, a true Strategist has enough confidence in themselves to know they have all the skills they will ever need, and any they feel they haven't got can be supplemented by others of their choosing.

3 STEPS TO BECOMING A STRATEGIST

<u>STEP ONE:</u>

Deciding that you need to become something that you haven't been before and that you are choosing this as a means to an end. A Strategist is unlikely to take entrepreneurship beyond their financial needs and will gain very little in titles like CEO or Founder etc.

<u>STEP TWO:</u>

Knowing that the majority of successful businesses in the world have been created not by Naturals but by Strategists. This means they are stepping into the majority.

Setting Up a Plan of Action. Maybe sitting down yourself or with others and making sure there is a direction with goals and 'achievables' outlined. This plan is likely to be altered, improved or even completely binned for another, but it's the map required to move forward without delay. As a plan of action it will contain an outline plus list of action steps. Having financials attached is essential and you may want to get a professional number cruncher in for this.

THE 10 STRANDS THAT MAKE A SUCCESSFUL STRATEGIC ENTREPRENEUR

1. IDEA FOCUS

When choosing to become a Strategic entrepreneur, you will be going forward with an idea in mind. Whatever this idea is, if you have taken your imagination there should be a strong feeling of wanting to make your business concept a money-making reality. Often armchair Reluctants will have a number of great ideas but no ultimate confidence to take things any further. Many others may be inspired and lack physical motivation to get up and get on.

The ideal type of idea focus is a form of obsession. It's a recurring thought or mental visualisation of what ultimately could be a new reality. After each new conversation with others, there will be the strong 'pull' towards something exciting and very feasible.

A word of warning is that talking in detail about your idea can be dangerous as business ideas are often pinched before they're even off the ground. Having a non-disclosure agreement (NDA) is one way of dealing with this, but is certainly never a watertight guarantee.

Ways of knowing if you've checked the idea focus box include having already made copious notes somewhere, even designs or rough sketches of your product. You will also have thought about your market, knowing that market comes first and product comes second.

2. JOINING THE DOTS

The second aspect - joining the dots - is about working out the journey from idea to potentially selling your business for a lot of money.

Once you can join the dots from A-Z you will feel much more confident and less likely to have forgotten something important.

As an example of all this in practice you may begin with a clear picture of your marketing and product and then decide to call in an accountant who can create some financials for you which also may be used to raise capital. The journey then starts to come together and you even know roughly what you are aiming for if someone came along quite soon with a blank cheque interested in buying everything from you. You may be surprised to know how common it is for only part of the plan being thought through and the rest of the journey being left to chance. This can only heighten the possibility of failure with the added pain of losing a great deal of start-up capital needlessly.

In joining the dots, remember to think about options at each stage. Giving yourself choices means that there are various roads that lead to your ultimate destination rather than one single track based on a 50-50 chance of success or failure.

3. REASON & PURPOSE

In any group of entrepreneurs, when asked the question: "Why are you in business?" the most common response would be to make a profit or to make money. This isn't very exciting when you think about it. Surely there are many other ways making money (profit), without some of the testing challenges that an entrepreneur will have to deal with. Your inner anchor as it were, is the main reason or purpose for you taking this direction in the first place. When things are tough, it's this reason that will make you keep going. Simply thinking of making money alone is likely to extinguish your original desire.

Probably for many people coming up with a good reason or identifying one's purpose is trickier than imagined. There are four 'purpose' choices here: *Need, Greed, Proud, Crowd.*

Need is about what's important to you more than anything else. Is it the freedom that success brings or having an on-going and growing cashflow? *Greed* is simply having more regular lumps of money to spend on things you choose. *Proud* is about self-achievement. Being able to prove something to yourself, and *Crowd* is about being a success publicly to the world at large. Fame and notoriety the important factors.

4. NETWORK POTENTIAL

Any good Strategic entrepreneur will develop contacts from a very early stage. Being able to have people to contact who can help in various ways is a big bonus although Initially there is no real reason to network unless you are investigating market potential.

Having a look at who is in your current database would be a good exercise. And once you get things going, getting into contact and exploring the people that they may know is always a smart move. The age-old quotation: "It's not what you know but who you know" should be ever mindful.

You could in fact make a checklist based on all of the occupations or business types that would be most valuable in your plans. Only then start to put a name next to each one of these. It will also instantly show you who you are missing and therefore who you should be searching for.

5. CAPITAL BASE

It's not always necessary to have lots of capital as an entrepreneur. In the book, "Growth Hacker Marketing" by Ryan Holiday, he explores the new trend in on-line business start-ups where the expensive marketing budget is practically zero. Here's what he says:

"Your new business went online yesterday and you've got a marketing budget of zero. How do you reach the first thousand – million – customers?

Enter the growth hacker. Growth Hackers thrive on achieving the impossible: creating something from nothing. From Airbnb to Dropbox, growth hacking has become a successful start-up's secret weapon, turning excited users into a viral marketing force..."

Yes, things have changed in the last 10 years and it's great to know that this is one of the best periods ever to make businesses work and wealth as a result.

And, there is something psychological about having some money in the bank. So what are the ways that you can raise capital? Here's a checklist you may like to consider:

- sell shares to people you know
- realise some of your savings
- use personal pension funds
- sell some things
- apply to the National Lottery
- find a 'business angel'
- a bank loan at a cheap interest rate

6. INTELLIGENT PERSISTENCE

The word persistence is often devoid of the preceding word 'intelligent'. In business, persistence as a solo concept does have limitations. The obvious one is being on completely the wrong track and destroying your business because you think persistence is more important than considering changing the way you are doing something that is not working.

It's a delicate balance between two separate concepts. Making a decision never to give up too quickly balanced with being smart enough to realise that the road you are travelling down has a very definite cul-de-sac. Being successful in achieving intelligent persistence will probably require discussions with others. Having at least one person in the discussion who is quite logical and another person who is much bolder and a risk taker might help you to squeeze yourself in the middle and better see what the best course of action is.

Of the downfalls in persistent only entrepreneurs is the desire to keep spending money on an ailing business quite regardless of the sense behind it. This often happens because of a feeling akin to gambling. The losing poker player wants to keep in the competition regardless of the money lost so far in the hope that things will turn around eventually and they will come out on top. This rarely happens in poker as it rarely happens in business.

7. Knowledge Access

In our information age, we are spoilt for access to additional knowledge. Though this is all good for the budding entrepreneur, the best knowledge comes from real people rather than virtual Google.

Spending some of your investment on consultants who are experts in the short-term is a good strategy. Perhaps you could even trade a few shares for reduced rates and fees? Never be afraid to negotiate whenever the situation presents itself. It's a great habit to get into.

Here's the knowledge checklist. There will be many more sources of knowledge and it might be an idea to create your own list as a matter of priority.

- legal
- financial
- accountancy
- social media
- business coaching/mentors
- patents and trademarks
- IT/websites
- graphics
- word smiths
- media creation
- growth hacking
- traditional marketing
- PR
- business gurus
- creative
- customer care
- HR advice

8. TRACK RECORD AWARENESS

When did you last give yourself a big pat on the back? The chances are you haven't done this for a long time and you certainly need to do it soon. A serious Strategic entrepreneur will be very aware that they have all the abilities required to go forward in a quest for the successful business. This may even be the case if they have never run a business before.

The idea is to recognise the success they have enjoyed in their life so far going right back to their first day at school. The more small successes they are aware of and can make a note of, the more likely they are to accept their latent potential in a manner that makes them supremely confident.

Track record awareness is often completely ignored and even deemed to be irrelevant. However, if you were to sit down to note everything you've done in your lifetime linked to success you may be very surprised and proud of who you actually are.

9. Flexibility & Open-mindedness

It's easy to talk about flexibility and open-mindedness but first a cautionary tale defining the three most 'dangerous' flexible entrepreneurs. Dangerous of course to themselves.

First there's the flexible type who is also over-generous. This individual ends up spending too much, asking for too little and hardly ever negotiating. Secondly there's the overly open-minded who continually goes off at tangents in any business discussion rather than sticking to what the meeting is about. Finally, there's the flexible and open-minded type that wants to keep re-inventing the wheel as it were. They are presented with ideas that are immediately re-drawn, re-designed or re-thought.

A good flexible and open-minded entrepreneur is thoughtful, takes plenty of notes, is keen to know everything that needs to be known and will proactively listen as well as ask good questions.

10. Gut Instinct

We all have gut instinct or intuition. It's wired into us at birth, and because there's no official handbook for the human mind it's something that has been overlooked by most of us.

In business however, going with gut instinct can be the difference between being unsure of what we are doing to being clear on what we should be aiming for and seeking to achieve. It also helps the Strategist stay away from those activities that zap energy, time and the will to live.

Key uses for business Gut Instinct include:

1 - First Impression Interpretation

When you look at a website, a brand, a business card and so on, you don't have to be an expert to know what works and what's not working at all. And it's your very first impression that tells you all. It's stepping back and thinking about something too much that creates confusion and loses that all-important gut feel.

Some senior managers in companies refuse to see the various versions of either brand or product until the item is ready to be officially unveiled. Then the wraps come off and they subject all the senses to what they are looking at so they can make an initial first impression decision.

On the whole this approach seems to work more accurately than any other way, and flies in the face of the idea that snap decisions are unwise. This is probably because we are not strictly talking about decision but a reaction or feeling. It's really worth investigating this type of instant interpretation. If you would like to explore this further do pick up a copy of Malcolm Gladwell's book, "Blink: the Power of Thinking without Thinking".

2 - The People Factor

When in meetings, interviews or general business interactions, going by your gut instinct will probably be more fruitful than being logical in your approach. Watching body language for example will tell you more about what's going on with someone compared with simply listening to their words alone. Being intuitive does require a fair amount of focus and diligent use of one's senses but can be done both face-to-face and over the phone.

3 - Product & Services Instinct

Entrepreneurs can easily become 'unhinged' in their thinking about products and services by stopping to see themselves as a customer first, entrepreneur second.

If you are not that excited by your product or service, then it's unlikely that others will be. There has to be at strong edgy feel when you handle a product or read about a service on offer. Get this right - often by gut instinct and you are flying.

4 – Cash Flow, Pricing & Money

Once again, you don't have to be an accountant to know how important cash flow is and that being blindfolded to the figures that underpin every business is tantamount to business suicide.

THE POWER OF THE STRATEGIST

When we are talking money, we are also aware that there is a certain type of individual with a defined personality that finds it relatively easy to turn a dollar into five hundred dollars in a short time frame. They don't necessarily have enormous intellect, nor do they have lots of business qualifications. (The majority of people who hold University degrees are not necessarily that wealthy). Being a strategist is a mindset choice. It's someone who knows what they want and is prepared to do what it takes to achieve it.

There was a story that was perpetuated in the 1980s about 100 people who graduated from Harvard in the 1960s… 25 years on. It went like this. Apparently, a group who all started out equally with a degree at age 22, two and a half decades later were in one of the following categories:

- Rich - 1
- Independently wealthy - 4
- Well off financially - 17
- Still Working - 64
- Dead - 14

These figures are reported differently, and sometimes with different categories but there is no actual formal record of this at Harvard, and some think it a great story created by a creative management consultant.

However, the key to this tale is interesting, because largely it does reflect what happens to people in their working lives. Of every 100 people, only 5% are likely to really make it money wise, and the reason postulated is that most people - the ninety five percent - rarely plan or shape their finances where a tiny number, five of every one hundred do just that.

This brings *the Strategist* back into focus again. And someone who has the features outlined or is prepared to take the features on board, is likely to be well placed for the acquisition of wealth and all that it would bring such an individual.

Character Notes and Steps

WHAT ARE THE MOST IMPORTANT MESSAGES?

ACTION IDEAS

ACTION STEPS – *MY COMMITMENT*

7

The Money Pitch

"How many millionaires do you know have become wealthy in investing in savings accounts? I rest my case."
Robert G Allen.

If you wish to get wealthier in your life there will be times when you need to pitch for money. This can be quite simply an interview with your bank manager, setting up a small business and requiring some capital from friends or even going on the TV show Dragon's Den and sourcing funds and friends in high places.

For dramatic purposes, some really poor pitches have been sanctioned so that viewers at home could cringe in a ball on their sofas. Those entrepreneurs who had time to do a little preparation, and provided they had a reasonable product, all went on to get finance and dragon support. There have been a fair number of success stories - and equally interesting, poor pictures that were rejected but based on very sound ideas that went on to great success. This really does underline the importance in being able to pitch for money.

Because when this is done well with a right idea under the right circumstances, fortunes can be made. Ask yourself the Question: right now if you had to pitch an idea for a small business in front of other people, how confident would you be in conveying a crisp and professional sounding message that hits the mark? Score yourself out of 10. If your score is less than 6, you really need to read this chapter. The fact is, if you can't pitch for money - you are relegating yourself to creating wealth in more traditional, mundane and quite frankly mind numbing ways - all of which should be avoided.

WHY PITCH IN THE FIRST PLACE?

Are there not Easier Ways to Raise Money?

The so-called easier ways to raise money are normally very expensive. These easier ways are like going online and applying for a loan, getting a new credit card approved and remortgaging against your home. Apart from a mortgage, the interest rates around these are normally quite excessive, they're totally contrary to money logic.

I say "apart from the re-mortgage route"… in my experience we all know at least one person who has re-mortgaged the family home to help put them in a position where they can make their business, idea or dream a reality and it can actually work!

On the other hand, there are various reasons why a pitch can lead to more money and a smaller interest rate where in some extreme cases such a rate is 0%.

Business Banks

It's probable that this type of pitch you have done before. Although today a lot of business banking and particularly loans is transacted electronically, there will be occasions when you need to pitch a business idea in order to get the relevant backing.

Pitching to your bank is also a good way to practice. If things don't work out there is potentially another bank you can try. If you're dealing with investors and those we wish to tempt in to buying shares in your business you tend only to get one shot at it.

British businessman Tim Waterstone has this curious tale to tell about pitching his original idea for a bookshop to his bank. It was combined with an exhaustive Business Plan - all of which ended up on his bank manager's desk. When he was eventually called in to discuss the matter, strangely his bank manager asked him to provide 10 copies of the business plan. Tim Waterstone saw this as a good sign and probably went out to a local printers to expedite matters. After all this trouble and expense he was eventually turned down, something he could not understand. He later found out through someone else at the bank that this unscrupulous bank manager had merely toyed with him. Apparently the manager was going on to a meeting the day of the interview to train his colleagues on creating a business plan. He needed to take the copies of Tim Waterstone's plan to show them *how not to write a business plan!*

So the other aspect of this, is not simply being able to do a great money pitch both verbally and in writing, its also about the ability to read the person or persons you are pitching to in order to ensure you are getting through to them effectively.

Here are the four rules to consider when pitching to a bank:

1. *Do not come across as desperate or over enthusiastic.* So if you notice that there is some interest from the person you're speaking to you should be more concerned with discussing the interest rate itself rather than questions about when you can get your hands on the money. Though it never makes any sense, banks want to lend to people who don't need money and not to lend to people who really do require it…

2. *Always have something in Writing.* This is about ensuring that you are able to provide something in writing before being asked. It doesn't have to be a full-blown business plan, though it should certainly be a single page showing some numbers for at least the first financial trading year. Banks and anyone lending money like to see these financial insights provided by you and they should be thought through thoroughly.

3. *Err on the side of Caution.* The bank will want you to be realistic rather than optimistic, even though optimism is surely a key factor for success. So water down projected figures and curb your enthusiasm for your start-up as banks will have seen the other extreme many times before where the majority of those lent to go 'belly up'.

4. Have advisors on board. What impresses an organisation looking at a start-up, is that they have some idea of what they are doing. So being able to mention your accountant, solicitor, financial adviser and other such professionals will stand you in good stead.

Pitching to a large number of people is one way that many movies are made these days. Asking for £3,000 from 100 people for a low budget movie can be quicker than trawling around for the full sum from one place - which often takes forever.

Similarly, this method could be applied to a new business start-up and in reality you can probably get away with asking for a lot less from fewer people. This increasingly popular method is known as 'crowdfunding'.

The thing to do is first of all decide on how much money you wish to raise and then double it. This should be the figure you are looking for. Most certainly you need a business plan and some financials that have been drawn up by your accountant or business adviser.

The way to begin selling shares is as follows:

- decide what your business is worth
- confirm the amount you're asking for
- work out the number of shares/share price with your business adviser
- consider creating a video as a shorthand message to pitch
- create a definitive list of everyone you are going to approach
- start at the top and work through the list
- you may wish to send something out to everyone first and indicate you're going to ring them in order to answer any questions they have
- allow people to buy shares for a relatively small amount of money.

You do of course need the flexibility to be able to tempt people to buy reasonable amounts of shares by offering incentives to larger shareholders. This really needs further discussion and thought with professional advisers.

DRAGON'S DEN TYPE INVESTORS

Tips for Pitching in the Den

The very successful TV series Dragons Den, entrepreneurs are asked to pick share ideas for investment. Here are the top tips that many of them fail to appreciate or simply have no knowledge off.

- Rehearse, Practice, Rehearse

It's all very well planning your pitch, but it's like a high dive for the Olympics that **has** to be right. Continual rehearsal and practice is essential for successful delivery. You should be able to deliver your pitch on autopilot as it were so that you are looking at your audience and working with them at the same time.

- Know your first three sentences

Very simple advice. Know off by heart the first three sentences of your pitch. This means that the most important element - the beginning - has the impact and is completely correct every single time. It's extraordinary how something so simple is really done in a Dragon's Den pitch scenario.

- Why, what, how?

In purely logical terms, being able to answer these three questions before they are asked is the sign of a well planned money pitch. Why are they listening to you? What have they got to gain? How will it all work? (always in that order - why, what, how?)

- Create Rapport from the Start

If you've ever watched Dragon's Den you will see how some of their entrepreneurial visitors alienate the Dragons from the start. So make sure you create strong rapport at the very beginning so that people are on your side. Until you get this aspect in place there is no point in talking about business whatsoever. It will fall on deaf ears. And rapport can be created by a simple empathetic remark served up with a genuine smile and a spoonful of honesty. And always be honest!

- The Numbers Speak Volumes

Who would go into the Dragons Den without the numbers fully thought through and memorised? Most do!

- Be Humble yet Confident

The business world likes confidence yet through the eyes and mouth of humility. People are easily confused between humility in confidence as if by choosing one you can't have the other. This is simply not true and both of these must be in the mix of your money pitch.

- Love your Product

Do you really love your product? Where is the evidence for this? Is it how you talk about it? How you relate to it? Whatever it might be that love needs to be there because it will engender confidence in you and your proposition.

- Don't be Greedy

Finally, a common mistake in the Dragons Den is greed. People expect large sums of money to head in their direction with a rather trivial amount of shares in return. Greed is not good and has no place in the money pitch.

PIGGY BACK

Probably the most overlooked area for raising money is from businesses who may appear to be competitors. The thing about businesses that are similar to your own, is that they totally understand where you're coming from, and therefore any serious opportunity that they should consider.

Piggy Back is about aligning with them so that they see opportunity with you rather than without you. Business giants like Google, Apple, Microsoft and Virgin have always been open to investing and or buying up businesses that complement what they are doing. Of course this is not exactly the same as pitching for money and raising capital, but certainly in the same ballpark. There are so many advantages piggybacking on an existing business which include finance, knowledge, experience and existing opportunities to the marketplace.

Another exciting aspect about piggybacking is that you can save yourself a great deal of time and chop a ten-year business into five or even two years in terms of profit extraction.

To piggyback successfully, make a short list of those businesses that are most like your own. Next find out as much as you can about them. Who are their principals? Can you get to them via LinkedIn for example? If not how best should you proceed in order to connect with them? The following information in this chapter should help.

Types of Format:

1 - Powerpoint/Keynote

There are a lot of derogatory things that have been said about PowerPoint over the years, however a PowerPoint presentation when done well can be interesting, provocative, and highly persuasive. Good presentations will have video embedded, quality graphics and a movie like quality. Do note however that when you are money pitching the people in the audience need to connect with you personally rather than an impressive presentation on its own. Whereas the two are important, you will take priority when they are considering whether they should get their cheque-book out or not.

Key Considerations include:

- - Keep it short.
- - Think story rather than random concepts
- - The quality of your visuals is inextricably linked to you and your product.

2 - Display Boards

Though this may appear to be going back into the past, display boards tell your story and can be quite successful because they will come across in a more interesting way then the expected PowerPoint route. Such boards should be made from stiff card, be colourful, fun and have a crisp message. The beauty of display boards is that there is no technology to go wrong, it is quite hands-on and therefore with some passion and conviction can make a good point.

3 - Spiral Artist's pad

This is another version of display boards, yet it is all housed in one place in normally a smaller sized format. There is also the opportunity to stand the pad on a desk allowing you to gesture as well as take notes.

4 - Video

Creating a good video clip is like constructing a television advertisement and we all know how powerful they can be. It will also show your true creative metal because rather like an advert, ensuring your message is creative will leverage your overall opportunity on successful outcome. People can also get quite mesmerised by video, taking the viewer into a world of their own - provided it is a well-made piece in the first place.

Any video should be quite brief and three minutes is a good guide. With today's smartphone revolution, the video could be made using your phone and there are various products online which allow you to edit the material with relative ease and professionalism. Videos may subsequently be placed on YouTube, Vimeo, Facebook, LinkedIn and so on.

5 - Audio

Audios are overlooked as a form of media, yet are equally powerful when compared with video. Once again, a well-made piece of audio media will take the listener on their own mind journey and therefore this type of method of money pitching can be extremely effective. Audios may be made on a laptop or smartphone, equally easily edited and music applied at the beginning and end. Do bear in mind that some people are quite visual and others are auditory. This means that they listen carefully when taking in information to make a decision and can be swayed by the tone and volume and speed of the delivery. These people are quite logical and analytical and will prefer to listen to something rather than look at something. Both audios and videos may be sent within an email provided they are not too long in length.

6 - Animation

There are more and more apps and software available to complete beginners in the creation of animating the messaging. The thing about animation is that it's easy on the eye, normally easy to digest the message, and quite watchable for most people. As a result using this medium for a money pitch is likely to lower the mental barriers provided it's part of the overall strategy in asking for investment. What should be avoided is spending excessive amounts on agencies or graphic designers which can be counter-productive and not worth the investment on your side.

7 - Website

For a few hundred pounds you could purchase a URL and get a web company to launch a very simple platform that professionally communicates your message and makes such a message accessible to anyone 24/7. There should be the all-important contact button where interested parties can get in touch. The other benefit with creating a website, is that it looks like a 'done deal' or going concern, even if the reality is that it is still in start-up mode.

Voice

How you sound does make a big difference. It shouldn't, but it is significant. If you have an unusual sounding voice that perhaps is too high-pitched for example, you may wish to consider all the money pitches to be done by someone else on your behalf. This is the importance of the voice.

Assuming you are happy with your voice, and more importantly others are, then your delivery should be measured, have clarity and overall sound amiable. People have to like you before they part with cash. The three factors around a good voice delivery is tonality, the right volume and speed of delivery.

Body Language

Whether we like it or not, your body language says a lot about you - and if you are unaware of this, you could be sending out completely opposing messages compared with what you actually want to say.

When pitching to a group of people, open palm gestures are recommended provided that they're not overdone. Eye contact is hugely important, and where a group is concerned ensure you are spending a few moments from time to time making eye contact with everyone in front of you. If this is a large group, then pick out different people to make some eye contact with throughout your pitch.

It's well understood that the folding of arms is not recommended - so open gestures rather than closed ones. Stay rooted rather than wander around while you are pitching. Although it sounds obvious do smile rather than look too serious all the time. Equally, telling trivial jokes for the sake of it is probably not a good idea when you are pitching for money. Your audience needs to take you seriously and therefore humour should be confined to perhaps something mildly amusing at the beginning and potentially at the end.

When taking questions ensure you look directly at the questioner and avoid interrupting. Listen intently, take note if appropriate and nod your head to ensure the person asking the question feels you are engaged.

Word Choice

When choosing the right words, simplicity will always win over complexity - and at the same time take care to avoid phrases and expressions that are too colloquial. Definitely avoid words like **cost** rather than **investment**. The language expressed needs to sound safe and ultimately for any money coming in your direction - in safe hands.

Dressed for Success

This aspect has to be the one that a small minority of people get completely wrong. Unbeknown to you at a subconscious level people are looking at the cut of your business attire, your shoes, choice of glasses if you wear them, the kind of pen you might be using (is it ostentatious indicating someone who can't be trusted with money or is it cheap and nasty which equally creates a bad impression?).

Where business dress is concerned, (and there has to be a good reason for casual dress) simply go with the flow in terms of current business fashion. Dress smart but not overly expensive. It's like turning up to the meeting in a Ferrari sports car - what impression might that give potential investors?

A Good Story

Finally in terms of tools, think about what your story is. Every start-up should have a story that you can share with investors. They want to know how you got to this point in time and where you feel you are headed from here into the future. Can you offer your story in a short paragraph? What about in a single sentence? And if you had to, what one word would you choose to represent you/ the business/ the future.

Money Pitching Psychology

There is a great deal of psychology when you pitch for money. Here are seven elements to consider:

It's Not about Your Need but their Opportunity

The way you come across from the moment you open your mouth should signal a great opportunity for the person listening. This has to be all about them and what they could gain and not about you. Otherwise, it would be like you are pitching for charity and that is a completely different animal. Why is this opportunity such a good one for them? What will they gain short, medium and long-term? How does this opportunity work in reality? What are the risks versus the rewards? (Needless to say, the rewards need to outweigh the risks!).

Time is Short

A bit like a thriller movie, the clock needs to be ticking in the background. The person or persons listening to your pitch need to get sense of making a fast decision. Failing to do so would mean them missing out. Perhaps you are going to offer a deadline to all would-be investors in this initial money raising period?

Any time limit should be long enough for those who need to reflect to do so and short enough for those who are interested to realise they must come to a decision without delay.

Always remember that you will create consternation if investors have to wait for any unnecessarily long period for paperwork that follows the sum that they have sent you. This would contradict your original message about time being important.

Short Term Return Aspect

In creating good strategy for a business and asking for investment, you will be more successful if there is a short-term return for investors. To ask people to part with money and for them to never know how long it might take to get a return is not a very attractive idea. However if you are able to demonstrate a way that the investor can attain a return however small after 12 months - and then perhaps staged returns with suggested dates. This is the food for thought needed to make investment more likely.

Special Treatment

A further aspect, is that feeling of being treated in a special way by investing in the business. This clearly never happened for Ron Wayne, in 1976 who as one of the founders of Apple inc. sold back his shares for $800 making a small profit. Today those same shares would be worth billions. The reason he parted with his shares is because he didn't feel special like the other investors. As a result he thought the cash would be better in his pocket than part of a business start-up by a bunch of young geeks.

What you certainly do not want is investors wanting their money back whether they are legally entitled to do so or not as it will be a big distraction for you. So do think about how you can make an investor feel 'loved' and special.

Paint The Future

The majority of new businesses are based on ideas around the present and rarely is the future thought through thoroughly. In creating your pitch you need to travel into the future and clearly see the potential in real time. This will help you to articulate good reasons why people should invest and trust your judgment. If you cannot see the future and you are basing everything on fate, then how can you get others to come with you on this journey? Once you have painted a picture of the future then do view it regularly so it is real and almost tangible. This form of mindset will help you immensely to transform those images into stark reality and success.

The Figures Say it All

If there is one small investment you should make it is that of time and potentially some money to create a really strong set of business projection figures. This is the oil in the engine and without it you will come to a grinding halt around raising capital.

Because people with money to invest are normally not stupid, be very careful in how you put the figures together and present them - which is why a professional helping you is worth investing in. Projections are exactly what they are - guesstimates. So, in doing this the figures must make sense and anything that is overly ambitious, presumptuous or massively optimistic will sink your dreams quite rapidly.

WHAT IFS?

Your Business Goes Under and the Investors Lose their Money?

Now let's look at the downside - the absolute worst that can happen. Quite simply this would be your business failing and all the investors losing out with you.

Though this aspect is negative, it should be considered because when you accept someone else's hard earned money you should be sure that they know what they are doing. This is not contradicting everything so far in this chapter, it's about creating a set of scales to balance out investment and risk. So for example if you are accepting a cheque for £5,000 from somebody you need to know that if they were to lose this sum, it would not be the end of the world for them. You certainly do not want to be accepting anyone's life savings unless their bank balance exceeds their requirements.

Taking this idea further, it's essential that a legal document is created for any sums of money you are accepting that spells out the risk factor. In the same way you would be asked to sign a disclaimer or consent form for the most minor operation under general anaesthetic. The risk of not waking up is extremely small yet every year this happens to a handful of people.

The Business Succeeds and the Investors get Greedy or Ambitious?
The upside of any business, is that it succeeds beyond the wildest expectations of everyone involved. This sounds brilliant but you will get shareholders who now want to take great advantage of the fact if they possibly can. So do ensure all your agreements, investor paperwork and information presented is entirely watertight.

In the same way you need to invest in an accountant, you need a good legal advisor, preferably one who is with you for the longer journey and therefore willing to charge you a reasonable rate rather than being there to bill you at the drop of a hat for as much as they can get.

If You Fail to Take Action?
The final what if is about failing to take action. If you know that capital is essential for the success of your business then being too reticent to forge ahead and pitch for money in the form of investment could be your biggest mistake ever. There is nothing more painful then future regret when you look back and think - had I chosen a different path my life today would be so much better…

Character Notes and Steps

WHAT ARE THE MOST IMPORTANT MESSAGES?

ACTION IDEAS

ACTION STEPS – *MY COMMITMENT*

8

Wealth through an Azumbler

"As much money and life as you could want…the two things most human beings would choose above all. The trouble is, humans do have a knack of choosing precisely those things that are worst for them."
JK Rowling

So what is an Azumbler? For the moment let's say it's a type of passive income stream. Something that can be created, easily maintained and with the potential of growth.

This could potentially be the most important chapter in this book for you to become better off financially in the shortest possible time. Does this sound intriguing?

Now, make no mistake that *get rich quick schemes* are 99% myth and 1% possibility. Yes, there have been schemes where you follow the instructions and becoming wealthy is the result. Yet almost without exception such schemes require an excessive amount of work and often the same amount of time and effort could also be applied to working insane hours in a fast food restaurant. The really 'attractive' schemes often border on illegality like the pyramid selling propositions in the 1970s which were finally outlawed. They were called pyramid because the early adopters made all the money and the late comers paid the price.

In 1969 a postal scheme thrived in the UK where you sent £5 to three separate people on a mailing address of 12 names placing your name on the end of the list and removing the top name. You then made three copies of the list, sold the list to three friends and got them to do the same. At some point money would start to roll in. Apparently, the possibility was to make in the region of £1,875 which in 1969 was a king's ransom. The scheme was water tight, but for everyone investing to win, there would have to be an endless number of people on the planet with £15 to invest.

DITCHING THE DEMONS

In creating a method to constantly generate money there are dilemmas and often old voices in your head that need to be dealt with in the first instance.

- They say that there are no *easier ways* to create wealth
- It's not possible for *anyone* to create a means of creating a passive income stream
- My family have never been rich, so why could I suddenly become an exception?
- There would surely be a need to have a great deal of investment capital?
- Can I take the disappointment of trying and failing?

Yes there are many potential mindset distractions to creating an Azumbla, and those listed are a handful of hundreds of thoughts that will surface as soon as you start contemplating such a venture. But the bold will always reduce their chances of failure and the uncertain almost always find themselves in a dead end.

Let's look at an analogy. You're leaving a major city by car and you are in the slow lane of a three lane motorway where traffic is slowing down - especially in your lane. Then a road sign indicates that the reason is a reduction in lanes from two to one exiting left out of the city, where traffic exiting to routes right out of the city have normal traffic flow. This is why the fast lane is flowing normally and your lane is forming a long queue.

In this scenario you have a choice. You can join the long queue like most of your fellow motorists who seem resigned to their fate to wait, or you could join the fast line and push in just before the left lane merges into a single one. There will definitely be some vehicles that will do this of course. Most will receive the wrath of those patient road users who wish to wait and not push in. But what if you had a genuine reason to get to your destination as quickly as possible? It's dilemma time.

In a business scenario, pushing in could be equated to selling things at an unfair mark up, or making use of your customer base to get rich quickly at their expense which for most honest people is something that cannot be countenanced and quite rightly so. But is there a middle ground to this motorway scenario? Something that is relatively acceptable though does require taking a small risk and certainly not wanting to be overtly pushing in?

Let's come back to the motorway again. Okay, you're in the slow lane. If you were to join the fast lane and move at the speed limit to where the road splits either there will be no gaps to get into the left lanes and because you are not about to push in you will be forced to go in a different direction and then have to reconfigure your route from there or perhaps even do a U-Turn and come back to join an even longer queue. Equally, there is a high possibility that there will be an adequate opening for you to signal left and move into the left lanes without having to rudely push in. (Isn't this the same thing? - you may be thinking. Hold this thought). So given there is a gap, you signal left, get into the fast left lane, and then do the same to get into the merged lane that takes you out of the city. No other drivers have sounded their horn, flashed their lights or shown any animosity towards you. In fact no one has probably even noticed. Yes you were 'lucky' that there was a gap, but you had decided at the outset that you would not do any pushing in tactics and unless there was a reasonable gap to gently ease across, you would have to overshoot and go off in a completely different direction - which is part of the risk you are taking.

In real life, certainly in the 'developed world', people seem to prefer to do things 'the right way'. People who use their imagination, creativity and courage are frowned upon. In fact such people who go forward and thrive are probably not liked usually through jealousy. Excuses for the actions of successful entrepreneurs are 'luck' or 'right place, right time' or 'they had help from their family/others' and so on. The true reality is that all of us are always in the right place if we were to stop and properly see the wood from the trees. We are all lucky because the word 'luck' has been created on a total myth.

Of course sometimes we see people as lucky if they win the lottery. But those people didn't get £4m sent to them by chance. They will have been playing the game for a long time probably which increases their chances, and even if it was their very first ticket purchase, without that decision to buy a ticket, part with the money and be in the draw, they would not have won. Of course you may argue the many examples of people who appear to do nothing and gain wealth from nowhere but it always comes back to that individual having made decisions that have set themselves up for the 'luck' to being bestowed upon them. And there is a much more important consideration. If you believe in luck and not yourself you are probably in the wrong mindset for increasing the foliage and growth in your 'money garden'.

In the motorway dilemma example, all those resigned to slow down, queue and not think creatively want to do things the accepted way, and yes sometimes there is a stark choice between accepted and unacceptable.

Most of us would want to choose the former. But the summary to all of this is - if there was a way of being creative, pushing yourself forward where you were not harming others, yet getting ahead because you simply refuse to slow down and choose the 'normal way' of doing things…could this be the essential mindset of a person dedicated to creating a better lifestyle for themselves, family and all those around them? The alternative is clear. Don't step up, don't think of having more money in your life. Because the creation of an Azumbla is stepping out of the crowd. It's turning your back on 'normality' and the usual way of doing things. It is being bolder, more imaginative and choosing to show more personal courage with your integrity fully intact.

Why do you need an Azumbla?

It means the idea of an additional or even more exciting - a sole passive income stream - requiring minimum effort. One of the prerequisites of creating an Azumbla must be that you really want this. On a score out of 10 where 10 is maximum passion for this desired outcome, the score of 9 is insufficient. It's like asking a lottery ticket holder for a score out of 10 for scooping the top prize. If they answer 9 or lower - why are they wasting their money? They'd be better off saving the money and certainly never complaining when they lose each week. And there's another idea. One way of financing your Azumbla if it needs a little seed capital is to save lottery money, save spending money on coffee, save spending money on nights out. It will certainly mount up quickly!

If you were to google *Azumbla* it's unlikely that anything comes up because it's a purely fictitious word created for this book to create a short hand term to explain a concept. Who knows, if lots of people create Azumblas it may make the mainstream!

An Azumbla is also another term for a **money machine.** Imagine each morning waking up, reaching for your smart phone and checking your Azumbla linked bank account to find that an additional £5,000 has come in as a result of worldwide overnight sales. How would you feel? For most people even £500 or £50 would probably put a smile on your face. The thing about this concept is that it doesn't have to be about a telephone number sized income overnight. It's about creating a small hole in the dam that trickles with the potential of the dam bursting in time to come.

HOW DO I CREATE ONE?

Now we are getting on to much more practical issues and for the purposes of demonstration we are going to consider the internet as a platform for an Azumbla. This could be an app or a website. Terror may have just struck you with the thought that you have no background or understanding of things technological, but this is only an example and we can look at non-tech Azumblas also.

SETTING OUT TO CREATE YOUR AZUMBLA IN 8 STEPS

1 - Brainstorm

Some would argue that this is the most challenging part of creating an Azumbla, and it probably is. There are many people with cash who are eager to put it into a great idea because in life there isn't a shortage of money but there does tend to be a hunger for a solid idea that will attract buyers. This is why there are so many charlatans on the internet ready to steal from unsuspecting buyers because they simply haven't got anything exciting enough to offer legitimately. However the counter to this is that after reading this book in its entirety the chances are you will be able to come up with an idea for your first Azumbla, and many more to follow hopefully.

The ideal way to go about the brainstorm is the use of more than one brain. It might be that you still end up with your own idea that you take forward, but other minds on the case would provide sounding boards which is a great filtration process.

Pre-Brainstorm Questions you may ask yourself

- What skills do people compliment me on?
- What skills do I most feel confident using?
- What business contacts do I have?
- What ideas have I had about starting a business in the past?
- Who would be willing to attend a brainstorm session with me?
- What would I love to do that also makes me money?
- If I could own any on-line/digital business in the world which one would I choose from an interest in that business (rather than financial) perspective?

- If I could create any product or service on-line/digitally and knew it could not fail, what would it be?
- What products or services online attract my attention normally?
- What would be the purpose of an online business? Purely to make money? To give me something to focus energy into and enjoy?

BRAINSTORMING YOUR AZUMBLA

This important creative meeting should be held in a location that will inspire. There should be no links with anything like home or work (your day job), and locations could include hotel lobbies or the hire of a small room. Some quality coffee shops will offer you a meeting space for free - provided you buy coffee. For example in the Leeds City {large well known brand} coffee shop you can ask for a proper meeting room which would normally cost a couple of hundred pounds in a plush hotel. There are others like this around the country.

At this session with the right people present, you need to take your best possible shot at creating the perfect Azumbla for you. Bear in mind that it's all about *market first, product second,* so an idea that sounds incredible still needs some basic market research to check the idea has 'legs'.

Depending on who is present, you may wish to ask people to sign a confidentiality agreement for the session. Imagine an amazing idea surfacing and others in the room desperate to go off and do it themselves...

2 - Focusing on The Product

Once you have a basic idea for your Azumbla, it would be an idea to start polishing it. Look at the finer details around it and does it pass the $X=Y$ formula where X represents the offering and Y represents value to the buyer.

TAKING YOUR CREATION INTO THE DRAGON'S DEN

Of course this isn't a literal suggestion (not unless you really wanted to, in which case you should go to the BBC website). This is about imagining you going up the stairs or elevator to meet five successful multi-millionaire entrepreneurs in order to pitch your product for investment. Imagining that you really had to do this, it would be a great exercise for you to work out what you would say and be clear about benefits, return on investment and financials. Such clarity can only make your offering more real in your own mind, and also see what the shortfalls might be.

DRAGON'S DEN CHECKLIST:

- do I have a good name for the product?
- does it have a brand that's distinctive and appropriate?
- can I summarise my product in a single sentence?
- Can I list the top 3 benefits?
- Do I know the market? Is there a big enough market?
- What are figures for the market?

- What are the next three years trading figures?
- Do I have an idea what value I would place on the business in 12 months?
- Why am I setting the business up?
- What are the benefits for potential investors?

3 - Finding the People to Craft your Azumbla

Today, Google is the equivalent to the *Yellow Pages* of yesteryear. Now care needs to be taken as simply choosing the top hit isn't necessarily the way to go. Ideally getting a recommendation from a friend or colleague is your best bet, and in order to do this you need to be able to network.

If you are using Facebook, or even better, LinkedIn - these social media resources could be a good way to get started. Of course there are many companies and thousands of individuals in the world who say they can create apps and websites. Seeing working examples is of paramount importance and also asking to connect directly with satisfied clients is quite important if you don't know them. There are also opportunities to use escrow account services where the money is only transferred when you are completely satisfied. By the way, be aware that some companies will want to retain the source code on software and apps, and others are happy to allow you to have the source code as part of the agreement. Choose the latter if at all possible.

When choosing services, do negotiate. Where a good resource business will not come down on price, consider agreeing to 80% and paying the additional 20% if they stick to the agreed timeline. Of course all this needs to be in writing.

Cheap Tools

You may be surprised to know that you can pick a whole range of products and services to create a product from www.fiver.com. Each service is actually $5 US! This includes design and even simple programming, though rates can vary on something more intricate, however much cheaper than going straight to an established software design company or graphic designer.

Another place to look for word creation is www.lance.com. Many entrepreneurs including Richard Branson and Paul McKenna attest to the fact that word creation is not at the top of their skill set top ten. Being able to find someone who can create words for a relatively small amount of cash is certainly worth exploring and considering.

What about high quality video clips and royalty free music? Here you may like to visit www.videoblocks.com or www.audioblocks.com. For a relatively small amount of money per year they will allow you to use video and audio clips within any video sequence. By finding a freelance video editor, this resource will certainly keep your bills down. If you wanted to screen record by way of a demonstration to potential customers, consider *easy screen record* which is free or a small fee if you wanted the upgrade - available as an app. For those a little more courageous you could also consider *videoscribe*. This animation creation tool can be trialled for 7 days, and is meant for anyone as opposed to those with a technical disposition. Often animation is an immediate attention getter.

4 - PLAYING WITH YOUR NEW BABY

Once you have created the first version of your Azumbla you need to play with it and get friends to test drive it too. Make a long list of things that *don't work* as well as *improvements*. The main thing to bear in mind is that time is at a premium with launching an Azumbla, so be careful not to take too long over this. There is something called 'feature creep' with programmers. The buyer comes back again and again with requests for 'tiny' improvements which can end up being twice as much work for the programmer and outside the scope of the contract.

Yet even if you have friendly web or app creators who are willing to overlook such things, the more you look for perfection, the longer you are not making money… It is so very easy that in your desire to make an Azumbla, you shoot yourself in the foot by continually seeking to create the ideal product. With apps for example, the chances are your app will need a review/refresh/upgrade within a year or eighteen months tops, so it's better to get your product out there rather than waiting for the perfect product. Get some cashflow established.

5 - PUPPY DOG SALE PRINCIPLE

Trial a puppy over the weekend from a pet store, and the chances are you will want to keep it by the Monday. This classic sales principle is at the core of 80% of all apps out there. The majority of apps today have a free version. If the app is good and useful, there will come a time when the user wants the full blown version, often called PRO. This is where the app owner will make sales. Yet imagine if your app had been downloaded by say 10,000 users in the first year. If 2% decided to 'go pro' then this is 400 sales. If the app is .79p, your profit will be around .40p before tax or £160. Assuming you invested up to £10,000 to create your product, how would you feel after a year's trading? Clearly a more exciting strategy would need to be at the heart of your product.

6 - DOING THE STRATEGIC CALCULATION

A way to have clarity on how to make your Azumbla pay is work out up front what you want to create in your first year and then judge feasibility. If you make more - you'll be over the moon, but the last thing you need is a feeling of failure based on building castles in the sand. What would be best case and worst case scenarios? And how do you derive these numbers?

This is no straight forward matter and you need to seriously get a feel for how popular your idea is. If you have a good concept and others have said so rather than you think so, then a free download will be achieved by word of mouth. In order to get that you may wish to get 10 people you know with large Facebook/Twitter and or Linkedin accounts so that they can send a message to all their contacts of how good your product is. If you want this done in a serious way, you may need to get these 10 people in the same place at the same time and impress them with your product, perhaps even wine and dine them as it were. If they collectively have 20,000 contacts, then you may get 600 downloads initially and then say 50-60 a month thereafter as a worst case scenario. With some effort you could have 2000 downloads in the first 12 months. At a 3% take up rate to PRO, it's now best to think about what an upgrade would be charged at. If it was say £28 as a one off, sales would be £1,680 before tax. Not that exciting.

So you may wish to use the *Goldilocks Principle*. In marketing, when offering a product, having three options, a bit like Goldilocks and the Three Bears, an option that's cheap, one that's perhaps expensive and a middle option that seems just right would help people to decide faster. Most go for the middle one, like Goldilocks did. And you get customers the lower and upper end choosers too, though in smaller quantities. Let's say option 1 is £21, Option 2 is £54 and option 3 is £76. Of course people need to see the value of all three options.

Now let's look at a more positive possibility. Say 50,000 downloads in the first year based on some regular advertising, free blog reviews and lots of networking. 3% of this number at the middle option is £81,000.

The two crucial figures here are the number of free downloads and the price of the middle option. In the market place fairly simple products like the TO DO app called *todoist* is priced at around £18 per year where a youtube downloader is nearer £56. So if you like the financial formula of 56 x 1500 then both these figures need to be close to reality. You can in fact play with these two parameters. Is it more like 36 x 2400 or 69 x 1200? Ultimately you can work it back to your target download total and your pricing. Oh by the way, remember fees to the on line stores that hold your product which are typically a percentage of your revenue subject to a minimum.

7 - THE 4-HOUR WORK WEEK

Tim Ferriss is the author of "The 4 Hour Workweek". A good place to visit to start with is the website at *fourhourworkweek.com*. In the meanwhile here is a glimpse of this great resource.

Whether you're an overworked employee or an entrepreneur trapped in your own business, The 4 Hour Workweek is the compass for a new and revolutionary world. Forget the old concept of retirement and the rest of the deferred-life plan—there is no need to wait and every reason not to. Whether your dream is escaping the rat race, high-end world travel, monthly five-figure income with zero management, or just living more and working less, this book is the blueprint.

Tim Ferriss teaches you:

- How to outsource your life and do whatever you want for a year, only to return to a bank account 50% larger than before you left
- How blue-chip escape artists travel the world without quitting their jobs

- How to eliminate 50% of your work in 48 hours using the principles of little-known European economists
- How to train your boss to value performance over presence, or kill your job (or company) if it's beyond repair
- How to trade a long-haul career for short work bursts and frequent "mini-retirements"
- What automated cash-flow "muses" are and how to create one in 2-4 weeks
- How to cultivate selective ignorance, create time—with a low-information diet
- Management secrets of Remote Control CEOs
- The crucial difference between absolute and relative income
- How to get free housing worldwide and airfare at 50-80% off
- How to fill the void and create meaning after removing work and the office.

The 4-Hour Workweek also includes the sample e-mails, voicemails, and real-life deals you will need to master the new world of luxury lifestyle design.

Who is the author?

Timothy Ferriss, nominated as one of Fast Company's "Most Innovative Business People of 2007," is author of the #1 New York Times, Wall Street Journal, and BusinessWeek bestseller. The 4-Hour Workweek has been sold in 33 languages and has been featured by more than 100 media outlets, including The New York Times, The Economist, TIME, Forbes, Fortune, CNN, and CBS. Ferriss speaks six languages, runs a multinational firm from wireless locations worldwide, and has been a popular guest lecturer at Princeton University since 2003, where he presents entrepreneurship as a tool for ideal lifestyle design and world change. The reason this is such an important additional read is that it's packed with ideas that can help develop your Azumbla with minimum investment and maximum impact.

8 - Licensing to Sell your Azumbla

An additional way to make money is to license your Azumbla to others who would love to sell it. The key is a water tight licensing agreement and inevitable legal fees would be applicable. Licensing could be done on a territorial basis or based on the actual platform that supports it. However this would only be appropriate if the Azumbla sells at the most fundamental level and therefore licensing may take a year or two.

Does the Azumbla have to be internet related?

The main benefit of an online/digital Azumbla is ease of sale. Of course there are other non-internet Azumblas and there are ideas that are already well known. For example if you rented a room or even a property and had a management company look after the enterprise you would have an Azumbla. Equally if you are an author of a best selling book or collect royalties on a song you wrote, these two are Azumblas.

Character Notes and Steps

WHAT ARE THE MOST IMPORTANT MESSAGES?

ACTION IDEAS

ACTION STEPS – *MY COMMITMENT*

9

Negotiating to Win

"Let us never negotiate out of fear. But let us never fear to negotiate".
John F Kennedy

Often the term negotiation is mentally linked to business and the average person assumes it's not a skill they need to learn or be competent in. This is far from the case. We should all be good at negotiation for our careers, with our friends and family and most certainly where money is concerned. It's easy to confuse negotiating with bartering. The latter is not negotiating because its focus is on doing a deal by exchange of commodities or assets based largely on monetary value where negotiation is about an endeavor designed to *add value* by the interchange of disproportionately valued commodities.

If we were to officially define the difference it would be: *"Barterers focus on the exchange of specific commodities based on their intrinsic value. Negotiators look at all of the aspects of a negotiation and seek to identify potential ancillary incentives or concessions that can be combined with the primary commodities to leverage perceived value and thereby create incremental value".* (How-to-Negotiate.com)

This idea around perception is key to appreciate how important negotiation skills actually are because the perceived value that a trained negotiator can produce will always motivate the other party to take action and make decisions that were up to that point 'not on the table'. If you think about the number of transactions you have entered into in your lifetime to date, they would account for a large number indeed. Most of these financial transactions will not require a negotiation or bartering position.

Going into a popular well established coffee shop for example to acquire a Decaf Americano means a set price and no matter how hard you bargain for a reduction, you are unlikely to get 20% knocked off. However it's the other 20% of transactions, normally when a larger figure is involved where nifty negotiation tools can save you sometimes very sizeable sums of money.

If you are 40 years old and have earned on average £30,000 over 20 years, that's £600,000. If 80% of that was spent on transactions, that's £500,000. Now take 20% of this sum for major transactions which is £100,000. If you were a skilled negotiator, the chances are you could have saved at least 25% of this sum or £25,000 by negotiating.

By the time you are 60, this sum would be £75,000. Add pay increments and the amount would be nearer one hundred thousand pounds. This figure is immense, and for most of us, it equates to what we give away in our life time by meekly accepting the terms of a transaction that's set by a third party by the use of their sales skills.

Some of the situations where we can pocket quite sizeable sums of money include:

- buying a house
- purchasing a car
- home improvements
- pay rises
- buying holidays and hotel rooms

If you watch house buying programmes on television, when the potential purchasers walk into the house and start saying how much they like it, it's probably costing them a hundred pounds per smile or positive comment. Of course it's a TV show. Now in real life, if we value money and having more of it, we cannot afford to play our cards as it were all over our faces. The poker face is definitely important if you are to go away and then come back with an offer or potentially a counter proposal.

This particularly applies to buying a new car. For some reason purchasers of new vehicles simply assume it's a set price. Of course - it isn't, and the amount of money car manufacturers make selling new vehicles to those who are reluctant to negotiate runs into millions of pounds every year.

The other thing about being a good negotiator is the respect it brings. Most people in business appreciate that negotiation is part of the sale, and provided there is perceived equity on both sides, it is a preferred route to creating a post sales relationship. The point here though is the extending of this to all of life not just business. For example you propose a lower price based on offering cash. This also now allows the seller to come back with a counter proposal - like 'buy two and you have a deal''. Beware however of slipping into a bartering situation by considering perceived value. What else can you offer or suggest that doesn't have a monetary value, yet adds additional value to one or both sides?

NEGOTIATION STEPS

A simple set of steps for negotiation could be:

a) Prepare yourself and do your homework

b) Start the negotiation and state your case

c) Be clear on outcomes and objectives for both parties

d) Agree on an outcome or outcomes where both sides win

e) Shake hands on a final way forward

f) Carry out what you have agreed to on the basis that the other side does the same.

Negotiation Skills Defined

Warm Up Skills

Going into a negotiation, however small requires some warming up. This could be as little as a 10 second clarification of your strategy before opening your mouth. It can also include confirming in your mind that you are not going to meekly accept what's being offered to you and summoning as much self confidence as you are able at the same time. If there are 3 Warm Up Skills, they would be:

ONE: Self Confidence
TWO: Clarity of Purpose
THREE: Fall Back Position

ONE: Self Confidence

Some of us are introverts and can find self confidence a challenge while others are extroverts and feel better placed to straighten their backs and sharpen their resolve before opening their minds and mouths in a negotiation. An easy way to exude greater self-confidence quickly is to relax and think about the benefit you are about to attain from going through a few steps to keeping more money for yourself. A quick way to do this is to imagine what you would see in winning, what you may hear and how it feels. This in effect provides that burst of good vibes that motivates you now to enact your plan. Often this also allows your subconscious mind to kick in and say what needs to be said. Over time, you will get better and better at getting into the right mindset and 'negotiation state' in order to win your position. Even improving your position and not getting exactly what you intended is still a win.

TWO: Clarity of Position

In every day life transactions, particularly the bigger ones, snap decisions can be extraordinarily tricky and also quite dangerous in terms of losing your money. Sometimes your shirt! So being clear in what your position is and the options that surround them is always an important factor. In such cases asking to have a moment to think about it is an excellent strategy. In the kitchen showroom for example, step out and go have a coffee somewhere and think hard about what your counter proposal should be. The person selling to you will largely assume you accept their deal or you walk away.

This is because the vast majority of retail customers never think about the transaction as a negotiation. This makes it even more advantageous for you to buck the trend. The sales person will always have some wriggle room and will want to use it to get a potential customer to sign up without delay. However, as a 'trained' negotiator yourself from reading this chapter and taking on board top tips and tools on offer, you can and will carve a much better deal clawing back potentially hundreds of pounds that you would have lost by being a shrinking violet.

Let's look at the new Kitchen Scenario.

Price: £11,162.20
Your Offer £10,150.00

Now List the intangible possible elements:

- cash payment by bank transfer
- recommend 3 friends post a good job done
- willing to give written testimonials
- willing to be a 'show home kitchen' in your area during work proceeding
- happy to use your social media contacts to send positive messages

Of course you need to do your homework on the supplier. Sending all the money upfront to a 'one man band' can be a highly risky thing to do.

However, if it's a well-known company, this is an option and by selling back the idea through negotiation that you can bring added value in the relationship, the offer price will always start to come down. I remember doing this many years ago with a new small car. I suggested they take off £500 from the asking price if I signed today and the sales person agreed immediately without batting an eyelid. At first I was delighted, but then thought that if it was that easy, what could I have got knocked off the price of the car if I had really negotiated?

THREE: Fall Back Position

'If all else fails here is my final offer' is something else that few of us are prepared to think about in buying something. The main challenge is in our own minds. When we like something - really like it - we focus on what we want to acquire and therefore become putty in the hands of the seller. It happens so often in house transactions. You fall in love with the house and then want to simply say yes to anything in order to live in it. Clearly this is a grave mistake and unless you are already hugely wealthy, it does require a mental shift in looking at the far bigger picture; your wealth and ongoing financial position. It's like the little child aged 2 shown a Two pence coin and a Five pence one. When asked which one they prefer, the tendency is to choose the former because it's bigger. The heart strings make the kid reach for the big round one. Think about this when you are being tugged by feelings that are getting in the way of sound financial judgment.

Going back to the kitchen example, it's about deciding on a fall back position. This could be wanting a minimum of £500 scratched off from the asking price or an additional £500 worth of products/features added to the overall offer - or you will move on to the next supplier. Happily in kitchens there are many suppliers. It becomes much more of a negotiation if the supplier is offering something few other suppliers are able to offer. In this case it would be time to use more powerful negotiation tools from your toolkit.

1. Creating Rapport

In a negotiation, it helps to create rapport, however be very aware from the start that the other party will also be wanting to do the same with you. This means you may be thinking you are doing a great job on them, when in fact they are thinking precisely the same thing about you. With this in mind, there is a middle ground that you need to achieve. In an ideal world, you need to give the impression that they have achieved their objective with you, but be focused on what you want, not what they are pushing you towards.

2. Good Verbal Communication

Do take notes. So often there will be something said that doesn't sound like what was previously discussed and so it's critical that you have something to refer to. This is the platform you would build your negotiation upon. Then when important things are discussed like features, benefits and figures, do repeat these back to the other party in the form of a resume or summary so there is no misunderstanding. Also saying things like, 'this is what I want from this' may sound overly direct, but it's far better than 'pussy-footing' around with soft speak and creating a blur at the edges of the communication.

3. Understanding Empathy

Putting yourself in the shoes of the other party is very useful. We will be looking at a tool called 'Perceptual Positioning' but for now simply realising that empathy in negotiation isn't looking out for the interests of the other party as you would normally do. Here empathy is about imagining what the other party would be asking, imagining or wanting in advance so that you are able to counter propose in the present. For example, being sold a car and putting yourself in the mind of the sales person.

Empathising from their side of the table would mean realising the following:

1 - they want to sell the car because this means a win for them

2 - negotiating will be par for the course and so they are open to it

3 - they are likely to flex a reasonable amount because you walking away is bad news. You staying to find an agreed way forward is good news for them.

4. Dealing with Barriers to Success

In a negotiation, there may be sticking points that get in the way of striking a deal. To focus on getting beyond these sticking points, always itemise those points which appear immovable barriers. It may be for example that you are agreeable to go ahead with the purchase of a car on all fronts bar one, the asking price. Being able to voice this persuasively and highlighting the fact you are close to doing business is very powerful. So something like this:

"Mr. Smith I am ready to go ahead with this car. I have agreed to a colour that you have in stock even though it's not my first choice, and also happy to proceed with the finance at what appears a higher than expected interest rate. I am also ready to put the deposit down now (credit card in hand) and agree to your valuation of my current vehicle which I did feel would have been worth a bit more. The only thing holding us back from doing business here and now is the asking price which you say you are unable to reduce. Should we at least agree on me taking a 10 minute break for a breath of fresh air and this will give you a chance to think about the price one last time?"

Can you see how persuasive this is?

Of course if there are more than one big barriers to success then start with the biggest one first and work down in a similar manner, however do deal with each barrier as a separate conversation and negotiation.

5. Playing a Good Hand of Cards

Once again, this is a negotiation trait that may sound complex or require a great deal of planning yet can be done on the back of an envelope in reality. It's about being clear of your advantages and those that the other party doesn't have.

As a rule of thumb, instant advantages in any financial negotiation includes liquidity of funds, time and timing, ability and desire to go ahead from your side and any other non-financial 'carrots' that can be brought to the table.

6. Dealing with Objections

There is a simple and effective way to deal with an objection in a negotiation. It's a three-step tool.

1 - Welcome the objection.

2 - See it from their side and tell them so.

3 - Ask a Question to move things on.

For example. You are buying a second hand bicycle where the price is £100. Having offered £80 the seller balks. Now use these three steps:

"I'm pleased in a way that you're holding on to your original price because it gives me confidence that the bike is in good condition. If I were in your shoes I would probably be thinking exactly the same. And - if we could agree on a mutually beneficial amount, would that be okay?"

Here, you are starting with a positive welcoming comment that pulls the other party in rather than pushes them away. Then there is a layer of empathy in the middle before asking a question to move things forward. Notice how it ends in the word 'Okay?' If a question ends in okay? The other party is most likely to agree provided the question is a reasonable one. Practice this three-step process as often as you can with family and friends. It may surprise you how really effective this is in reality.

7. Use of the Negotiator 'Toolkit'

Once you have got your head around the basics of negotiation, there is a toolkit you may like to dip into. Firstly, the three tenets of the Negotiation Model are *Outcomes, Variables and Gambits*. These are simply knowing ideal outcomes for both parties, gathering the variable information needed to trade and the easy to implement tools that cut any negotiation down to size and to your advantage. Let's look at the gambits now.

The Negotiator's Toolkit - 9 Gambits

These gambits or tools are broadly speaking covering four areas of negotiation.

Classic Concepts

These Classic Concept Tools should be borne in mind to help you get a stronger advantage in a negotiation.

Two-Sided Pressure

In any negotiation both parties are under pressure to win, otherwise there is no negotiation. This being the case, ensure you are in no hurry to make overly generous allowances or to give way prematurely.

First Offer Rejection

Do reject any initial offer made to you. The exception to this would be something you truly want where money isn't the issue. For example a house that you have fallen in love with where you are aware of other potential buyers. If you haven't got sufficient funds, then negotiate. If you have the money then you have to consider what you may lose by suddenly becoming a tough negotiator.

The psychology behind the first offer rejection principle is around the fact that it can actually alienate the other party. They will be thinking, I should have asked for more. Equally it will worry you, as you think: 'It was too easy. I should have offered less'.

Different Desires

In any negotiation, the parties involved will want different things around the one item being negotiated upon. This is important to bear in mind. The factors you may think important may have no bearing on how they are thinking, while the things you think unimportant may be crucial to the other side.

Pricing

The Flinch

Seen often, probably without realising, this sharp intake of breath can save you thousands. And to make it more powerful, just keep practising it whenever you can. Get given a price, think Flinch. See price, think Flinch. Price - Flinch. Until it's second nature. And here's the key to it. You should flinch even when the price is a good one. It's all about making this your default price reaction system that automatically requires a response from the seller's perspectives. It's what sets prices tumbling and crumbling in motion, and all it takes is that crisp, lisp sharp intake of breath that lasts a full one and a half seconds.

'You'll Have to do Better than that!'

This is the phrase that follows the Flinch beautifully. And though you know it's a ploy, the other party knows it's a ploy, it still works!

How Close?

This little known tool is an absolute gem. And so often in negotiating or selling we do the exact opposite. For example we say things like, 'So what's your offer?' "What are you prepared to go with?" and "What can you afford?" Instead, think of the number you prefer and simply ask: 'How close can you get to XX?' The psychology here is super powerful in many ways. It is getting the other side to imagine **your figure** not theirs. It's getting you to instruct their thought process as well as guide them to the right end of the negotiation scale. So when the bathroom designer says: 'It will cost you £1000 for my design'', and you were thinking more like £600, ask (after a flinch): 'I was thinking more like £500. Tell me, how close to £500 could you get?'' Do bear in mind that the next person who speaks is likely to be the one losing out!

TRADING PRINCIPLES

NEVER FREE

We've seen it in all the hostage negotiation scenes on TV and in films. In negotiating with the bad guys nothing is given away for free. You want pizza, then you release a hostage. And this is the bedrock of sound negotiating. Nothing is ever free. If you, the buyer realise that the seller would prefer you to pay by direct debit, then make it clear you're not too keen on that route. Then you have something to trade *in return for* something that you want from the other side. Naturally the thing you trade will be of similar sizeable importance, unless of course you have a whole gamut of items that the other party *would like from you that* equates to a significant price reduction or other key factor.

WRITTEN WORD

An experiment was done in Cleveland, Ohio. The main highway leading into the city had a huge sign painted on a bill board. It said: 'Cleveland is closed today'. Now this wasn't an official sign. It was a hand painted note as it were, yet scores of cars were pulling up on the hard shoulder, looking at maps and making phone calls. Of course it was a joke, but motorists were responding to something engrained in their psyche. As humans we tend to respond to things that are put in writing. Even if the note is unofficial!

In winning a negotiation, pulling out a press clipping, referring to a magazine article, pointing to a blog on screen or referring to some hand written notes that were scribbled just before you arrived is extremely powerful in a negotiation. People can't help but take on board what's written down. Almost as if it means that things in writing are true, yet things that are spoken are suspect. Whether buying or selling, this really does work.

THE AUTHORITY PLOY

This strategy is useful when you want to counter propose. It's about:

''I need to check with'' and then:

- my partner
- my son/daughter
- my banker/accountant/solicitor
- my boss
- my team
- my neighbour

…and so on.

This provides a sturdy 'out' to have a think, come back and remain steadfast because it appears your hands are now tied and you can't do anything other than stick with your position.

IMPASSE TOOLS

PERCEPTUAL POSITIONING

This great skill is uncommon. It originates from the world of Neuro Linguistic Programming (NLP) and relates to acting and creative writing in particular. However, there is one other brilliant application for perceptual positioning, and that's negotiating. It's primarily the skill of adopting more points of view than your own personal one in a very experiential way. The classic phrase that's often associated with this mental empathy is the quote: "Before you criticise someone else, walk a mile in their shoes first." However, in doing this, all you are doing is in fact empathising. The first aspect is your direct view on something, where the second aspect is from the other party's perspective. It's also about viewing something using different senses. How does this look, sound and feel? The third position, and the one key to negotiation skills, is where you become 'the observer' of both position 1 and 2. Here you are weighing up what you see and hear from the two negotiating parties but as a third person entirely. And here the magic begins, because by taking this perspective it's possible to see, hear and feel things that are normally totally hidden. Aspects and understanding that can give you the edge in a negotiation.

In summary, be clear on your perspective - position 1, now put yourself in the other's shoes - position 2, finally be an 'independent' observer - position 3 and see the entire picture. Then pick out what you need to do, say or change in order to gain the advantage.

SET ASIDE

The final two impasse tools are only to be used when things are not going well and there is a form of deadlock. The first option is the 'set aside'. You would appeal to the time spent so far between the two parties by setting aside the one thing, often price that is not agreed, taking the time to show that everything else is. Given both parties want the deal to go ahead for their own individual reasons it's getting the other side to appreciate what is about to be lost for want of some minor mental flexibility. This isolating the barrier strategy will invariably have the desired effect and prompt the party to lower their expectations, knowing that the only other option is…

WALK AWAY

Though a defeatist tool, sometimes it takes walking away to jolt the other side into changing or amending their offer. So be prepared to walk away, but principally as a ploy to effect a better offer.

Character Notes and Steps

WHAT ARE THE MOST IMPORTANT MESSAGES?

ACTION IDEAS

ACTION STEPS – *MY COMMITMENT*

10

Creating a Dream Business

"Nothing is, everything becomes, no condition persists unaltered, even for the smallest moment, everything is ceasing to be what it was, and is becoming what it will be."
Heraclitus of Ephesus, 400 BC

DEFINING THE DREAM

Most of us dare to dream for what we want financially. Have you considered that dreaming alone isn't enough albeit a step in the right direction? Random dreaming should ideally be shaped and nurtured in a slightly different way for the process to be useful and potentially produce a regular and growing income stream. For those who have been successful in transforming a dream into real time actions and a business to be proud of, one of the most potent factors was the regularity of making mental images of the end result - rather like a dream, but the vital difference was controlling the mental pictures rather than allowing them to appear haphazardly.

Over two hundred years ago, Englishman George Boole was born in 1815. He was a mathematician, educator, Philosopher and logician. He was also a dreamer. Without his visionary life, we would probably be less advanced today in our digital revolution as he laid the foundations for it. His legacy was:

Boolean logic, a theory of mathematics in which all variables are either "true" or "false", or "on" or "off". The theory preceded the Digital Age, with American Claude Shannon applying Boolean logic to build the electrical circuits in the 1930s that led to modern computers.

Though Boole was an academic and very intelligent, there were many other highly intelligent people of that time, none of whom came up with the ideas that sets him apart from the crowd so dramatically. He even had time to set up a school at the age of 19 and lived a relatively short life dying at age 49.

The moral of the story is that being a dreamer is a good thing, but only 50% of the requirement for financial business success. The other 50% is taking all relevant actions to transform the dream into a dreamy reality.

Negative thinkers who wish rather than dream with conviction always come up with excuses when it comes to taking action on ideas. The number one excuse is that all the best ideas have already been thought up - which if you think about it, is absolute nonsense. In fact Einstein was very clear that his forte was much more about creativity and much less about mathematics and intelligence.

- In short, make a decision on what you want to dream about
- Choose a business that you would love to get into
- Think about it at the same time once or twice a day for say 10 minutes
- As you deliberate on it, see and focus upon the fine details of the mental imagery
- See yourself taking the actions that lead to the realisation of the dream.

It may also be an idea to keep a record of your ideas in a 'Dream Diary' as it can be all too easy to forget a great idea. Review your thoughts in writing regularly.

The Purpose of a Business

In 1998, a group of 100 small business owners were asked by a well known American University two questions:

1 - What is the purpose of a business?

2 - What is the purpose of your business?

It's probably no surprise that the answers to both questions were slightly different. A massive 86% of the group felt that the purpose of a business in general was about making money and a profit. In respect of their own business the reasons were rather varied and included things like 'giving me something to do when I get older'.

Only 3% had started a business for altruistic reasons beyond profit alone. Let's examine these two questions more carefully. Probably, the purpose of a business isn't:

- making a profit
- employing people
- growing an empire
- starting a new trend that sells
- getting in on the digital age

What if we were to stand back and view a business as a product in its own right. If a business was in fact a product, would it help to determine what one should do with it? Surely the purpose of any commercial product is to sell it? So why don't we see this as the purpose of any business? The real benefit of this concept is that the business is likely to be better run almost immediately when you truly accept the notion. Because in order to sell it, it would have to run like a Swiss Watch and be a successful 'money machine'.

Now if you ask the two questions again, the answers are going to be exactly the same. The purpose of a business is to sell it, and the purpose of my business is to sell it. (Even if you never in fact actually sell it!) Think also about the purpose of buying a house is to sell it, even if you never actually do so. The fact you see it in this way means you will want to decorate and improve it, which means you'll end up living in a space you adore for all of the time rather than doing it up, loving the new space and living in it for a fraction of the time before it's sold.

CHOOSING A BUSINESS

This is an easy or difficult question as there is no middle ground. Deciding what business you want to be in is normally based on personal desires and values. Easy if you know what you want to be in, difficult if you don't. In the latter case, simply choosing any business doesn't seem a great idea, however in theory, if the purpose of any business is to sell it, it should be quite straight forward to pick a business at random and turn it into a saleable product. In reality, motivation, inspiration and the choosing of a relatively easy business will of course help you achieve your goal significantly.

THE 4 WAYS TO GROW ANY BUSINESS

Accountants are quick to point out the importance of numbers in any business and having sight of the balance sheet regularly, but few highlight the basics and that the entrepreneur needs to be aware of the 4 Ways to Grow a Business.

1 - To Increase the Number of Customers of the Type you Want

2 - To increase the Transaction Frequency

3 - To increase the Average Value of Each Sale

4 - To improve the Effectiveness of Each Process that makes the Business Work.

Increasing the Number of Customers of the Type you Want

In building a business, it's so easy to go for anyone with an open wallet or purse. Yet this unwise philosophy has been the ruin of so many businesses down the ages. Knowing almost exactly who your ideal customer is allows you to better target your success arrows and also know more clearly what your offering should be, a customer engagement strategy and where you should take the business in the future regarding potential new products and services. Of course this can be taken to extremes. There are companies selling holiday villas for example who will only let you look at them if you fill in an extensive questionnaire so they know you qualify for their customer profile. There are better ways of doing this and certainly more subtly as it does give the impression (probably quite correctly) that the company is only in it for the money.

Increasing the Transaction Frequency

How do you get customers to buy more often? This is about tempting them with offers in store or on line, not being concerned with the amount of the spend, but how often they transact with you.

Increasing the Average Value of Each Sale

When you're in a restaurant and they ask if you want to see the sweet menu, naturally they're seeking to increase the order value. What's more interesting is whether they are doing it as a habitual operation or as part of a financial strategy. Because if it's the latter, there are numerous ways of doing this, and the people who are serving, with a good appreciation of this, can make a big impact in a food service scenario. Every industry will have its own way of dealing with increasing the average order value, and what's important is being aware of its importance.

Improving the Effectiveness of Each Process that makes the Business Work.
The fourth business growth factor is about process improvement. In the latter part of the previous century, Kaizen became a popular concept from Japan. It means *improvement* and can refer to a small change or momentous one; on a regular basis or once only. Where there is no change, there is no improvement, and when businesses fail to improve, they normally fail to survive

STEPS IN SETTING UP A BUSINESS TO SUCCEED

STEP 1

The Concept
Probably the most exciting part of a business venture in order to grow a cashflow and subsequent on-going monthly profits, is coming up with that all important concept. This is easier than you think because new concepts are often built on very old ones. You simply have to be brave and bold. Examples of new concepts from old ones include Starbucks, Tie Rack (mainly in 80s/90s), and Subway. It's about a different way of packaging, branding and marketing. And do also consider being different about service, messaging and value to the consumer.

STEP 2

Market first, product second
A great product is a waste of time if there are potentially only 12 customers worldwide. Many entrepreneurs have had their fingers burned because they spent lots of money on the product and practically nothing on market research. If you ever watch 'Dragon's Den' you will see so many clever ideas that don't even get off the runway because there's simply no market out there for their brain wave product. Maybe the reason there's 'nothing out there like this' is because of that very reason...

STEP 3

Product/Service Completion
The third phase is finalising and 'polishing' the product/service. What makes it different from others in the market? Can you truly differentiate?

STEP 4

Business Strategy
Now it's time to put a business strategy together. The strategy should also end up as a business plan that anyone can read. This may include banks, accountants, potential investors and possible business partners.

Business Structure

How will you structure the business? Draw it out on a sheet of paper. Ask others for their opinion. How workable is the structure? Who will be doing what?

STEP 6

Make it Easy to Buy from you

As ridiculous as it sounds, many well know brands actually make it difficult to buy their products. This could be on line where the BUY NOW button is in some obscure place or on a totally different page! In a store, challenges to make a purchase include hidden cash desks, unmanned cash desks and the non-acceptance of cards like American Express. The business seems to prefer to lose an entire sale rather than pay an extra percent or two which, if you think about it, is madness.

Ease of purchase also includes an understanding that it is also easy to return goods that are faulty for a complete refund. There was a recent publicised case of a disabled man in a big brand British coffee shop who took one bite of a sandwich he purchased there, didn't like it, and asked to change it. It took a 20 minute painful debate by the manager who refused on the basis that the sandwich had been eaten. (That's one single bite). Ultimately, and although the manager finally agreed to the change, the incident had already been reported on social media which did the brand no good at all. Not a good example of making it easy to buy.

STEP 7

Regular Customer Engagement

The final step is creating regular customer engagement in the form of weekly or monthly blogs, communiques, mailings, adverts or whatever it takes within your budget to keep your message alive and well. Today almost any business can get good value from a thought through campaign and it's often less expensive than you'd think.

THE 4 ABSOLUTES

FIRST ABSOLUTE

Set Aside as Much Money as You can Muster.

It's less about how much, and all about your attitude to kick starting an enterprise with as much cash in your business account as you can raise. This also sends a signal to your subconscious that you are serious and you are embarking on something vitally important. If you were to regard it as less than vital, you can imagine how this might impact your overall success.

You may also wish to create 100 shares in your enterprise and sell part of the equity. However the sale of equity should be a last resort as it would be much more prudent to hang on to as much of it as you can.

Second Absolute

Have Knowledge on Your Side

Every successful business will have a team of professional advisers. It's a good idea to have these people on board at the beginning, and this can be without having to part with any money. Knowing that advisers are in place will promote confidence, and through contacts and perhaps some networking, the business could have a layer of knowledge resources to hand.

Third Absolute

Prepare for Better or Worse

Not all businesses struggle when they start up and despite some rather negative statistics about the longevity of most new ventures, a new business is like getting married; for better or worse, richer or poorer. Raising one's hands at the first hurdle is not an option for a true entrepreneur.

Fourth Absolute

Believe in Cable Cars

One of the biggest myths in making money through your own business is that it has to be an uphill struggle to start. This is nonsense. It's like wanting to climb a mountain where the main objective is getting to the top rather than the climb itself, but you are blinkered about having to climb the mountain as the only way when there's a cable car on this particular one. Provided you are acting with full integrity, why wouldn't you take some short cuts in making your objective happen sooner rather than later?

The E-Myth Revisited

If you want to further explore small business excellence, Michael Gerber's **The E Myth Revisited** is worth delving into. The log line is: 'Why small businesses don't work, and what to do about it...'

It essentially talks about a small business requiring three elements:

- Technician, the person who knows the trade and can do it (often happiest doing it)
- an Entrepreneur, often a futurist who looks ahead and aims for the stars
- a Manager, a detail loving individual who crosses 'i's and dots 't's. Someone who is an organiser and is able to make the business function.

In essence, most small businesses are started by a technician who has created a job, not a business, because the roles (they don't have to be separate people), of manager and entrepreneur are not covered.

One of the biggest concepts in the book is the 'IN/ON Principle'. This is about working 'on' your business not 'in' it. Something that the technician loves to do and often does do from day one. Of course when it comes to sell the business, there isn't anything to sell.

Take the Printer. This man sees himself as a business, but when he adds up all his assets after 20 years and takes away debts and liabilities has a net worth of £22,000. This is just over £1,000 a year he has been working for. However, had he treated his business as a product from day 1, his actions, attitudes and business behaviours could have made a massive difference to that 20-year review figure.

THE PEOPLE FACTOR

Power to the People

Having the right people in your business may sound obvious but it can be one of the biggest challenges you face. A consideration is employing someone on a self-employed basis, but this could never be full time for tax reasons, so may not be an option. If you have to employ, check out the legalities, which today can be a minefield. Small businesses that suddenly have considerable out-goings from monthly salary bills can be over onerous and should be avoided if feasible.

So imagine you have decided to go into retail and you are going to employ a couple of people to run it. Of the many key traits, attitude and behaviours would come very near the top. To know whether someone is suitable consider finding out the candidate's *purpose* in wanting the vacancy. Such a question should exclude all financial considerations, as anyone who comes to work purely to pay their bills is unlikely to do your business much good. If you get a financial response then press further. Why else do they want to be selected?

People Profiles

There are generally 4 Types of Candidate. If you wanted to go into greater detail you could google Jung's Personality types 1971. For ease they are generalised here in a slightly different format.

1 - THE DRIVER: someone who is direct, wants clarity, speaks their mind and will be candid.

Interview Tips. These tend to be natural leaders and are good to have on board in order to get the most important jobs done.

2 - THE ANALYST

Analysts are useful to balance things up. They like to consider and reflect before making a decision and use logic in tricky situations rather than go with emotions. They will invariably be at home with numbers and seem to eat the more mundane tasks for breakfast as it were.

3 - THE ENERGISER

The life and soul of the party, this individual who is usually extrovert is able to add spice to situations, teams, creative sessions and PR for the business. You need at least one such individual early on in the business.

4 - THE HUMANIST

Normally an introvert, this person puts people first which is of course a good thing, but can sacrifice profitability by not being as focused on the business basics. If you need to set up a Human Resources element to the company, this person could be a good choice. They would also be useful if your product/service is people focused in a big way like a private ambulance service for example.

The three things that motivate people in reverse order are:

3 - Money

2 - Respect and Recognition

1 - MAD Factor or 'Making a difference'

This is born out from decades of research by business psychologists and where number 3, money, is not a surprise, many would think it should be higher up the list. In fact more people get greater motivation from the respect and recognition of others. More people would prefer to wear a branded top in public than have the money instead in a savings account.

At number 1, the MAD Factor stands to reason. The majority of people get the maximum motivation in making a difference in their own lives as well as the lives of their partner, their children, colleagues, the business and so on. If you consider some of the richest people on the planet, particularly movie stars and music legends, their driving motivation was through number 2 and 1 on the Top Three list rather than money.

What all this means is that you should use this knowledge when dealing with people in your business. People on the whole value genuine feedback, but there's an overlooked tool called *Soulfood*. This is like feeding someone's soul and should follow three principles remembered as GPS.

Genuine

Positive

Specific

When giving soulfood to one of your team which should be often, offer a comment that's totally genuine, one hundred percent positive and very specific about one thing. You may practise doing this with your partner, family and friends. It will also give you a big buzz and is highly motivational all round.

THE TRAITS OF TOP ENTREPRENEURS WHO DARED TO DREAM

In an article by columnist Rebecca Burn-Callander in the Telegraph, she cites top habits of Successful Entrepreneurs. She states:

It's a question that has been debated by academics, venture capitalists, economists and psychologists for centuries: what sets entrepreneurs apart from other people? Is it their appetite for risk-taking? Are they more ambitious or determined? What traits can be adopted by individuals to make them more entrepreneurial?

Here are some summaries of the traits she discovered from her research.

1. INVEST MONEY TO MAKE MONEY

This is one that is a deal breaker to many would-be entrepreneurs. They want to make money but don't want to let it out of their grasp at the outset. Worse still they penny pinch where investment into the business is concerned and take the opposite view when taking out dividends are concerned.

2. OVERWHELMING SELF-BELIEF

Jason Lemkin, a partner at Storm Ventures believed in his concept enough to put every penny behind the idea.

"In my first start-up, I had to sign a $750,000 personal, full-recourse note to get the company started," he says. "Start-up times were tough in 2002. If we hadn't gotten our first customer shortly thereafter, I would have lost my house, my car, my savings, everything I had. Was this a smart move? No. Not in any sane world. I didn't even tell my wife about this promissory note.

"But it was a good idea, a low-risk idea, because I could clearly see the other side. Everyone else said it was a terrible idea, impossible but 13 months later we sold the company for $50m to the same company that refused to buy us 13 months earlier for $50,000."

3. SELF RESTRAINT

Delaying gratification is a sure fire trait of genuine entrepreneurs who can see the big picture - the ultimate goal. Typically directors starting a business want to invest in expensive cars and office furniture, but this is often a big mistake. It's like going into a desert not knowing when you will reach the next watering hole yet drinking half the water supply after the first few miles.

4. SPOT SOLUTIONS NOT PROBLEMS

Those serious about business success let nothing come in their way. Obstacles are cast aside by thinking though, around and over barriers to success. It's less about outlining what's not working and all about strategising a solution and way through the maze. Richard Branson tells many hair-raising tales of how he was so close to losing his business on down turns in the market and it was only his resolve and dogged solution thinking that got him through.

5. UNCERTAINTY IS CERTAIN

Businesses are uncertain terrains and if anything is predictable it's not being able to one hundred percent rely on anything or anyone. Such an 'environment' will put many people off, yet the mind of an entrepreneur is simply, 'It's okay, I'll figure it out".

6. Learn Skills that are Worth Money in the Real World

Entrepreneurs think of their own skills as an investment. So whatever time they put into the business it should reap a significant return. They go out of their way to learn and are typically self taught in the skills they need to become successful and wealthy.

7. A Sense of Urgency

The entrepreneur wants to get from A to B in the fastest time possible. He/she wants the motorway. The non-entrepreneur will want to prevaricate, take their time, think about things and take the scenic route B road.

One way they get a sense of urgency is to live and breathe their idea rather than switch off every day at 5pm. But then, this also normally means that they are enjoying the journey as opposed to resenting going into an office where they have to leave their own values and ideas at the door and take on the mantle of someone else's in order to earn money accordingly.

8. Cost versus Value

Whatever they do, entrepreneurs think about time spent versus money. If time can be saved that makes a big difference on the outcome, they will spend the money gladly.

The non-entrepreneur will buy a standard ticket on a full train, have to stand for a two hour journey and arrive 'crumpled' where the entrepreneur buys a first class ticket, works throughout the journey, and arrives raring to go.

In a Nutshell

Wake up and start dreaming. Provided you action those dreams, keep dreaming, keep taking positive action and grow a fruitful business money tree as a main source of revenue even alongside an existing employment.

Character Notes and Steps

WHAT ARE THE MOST IMPORTANT MESSAGES?

ACTION IDEAS

ACTION STEPS – *MY COMMITMENT*

Part Three

H A N D S

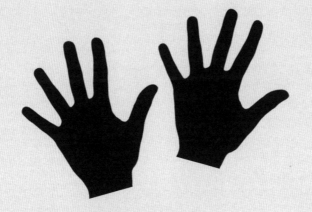

*Rolling your sleeves up, taking action, making it
happen, following a set of steps...
Growing Your Own Money.*

11

Getting Your Money-Hands Dirty

I have really been looking forward to writing this section. To re-cap we have looked at your Money Heart, explored ideas for your Money Head and now we are getting down and our hands dirty with suggestions for success by using your Money Hands. *Heart, Head and Hands.*

Here then is the 'What?' and 'How?' part. Provided you still have the 'Why?' with your accompanying notes from the first two sections helping to make things crystal clear, then we are both in a great place. Me, your guide, you the 'player' on a sports field of your choice chomping at the bit to make it happen.

At the very start of the book I explained how important mindset was for me and the following chapter will cover that. There's also a small piece on money management that many people who feel they have sufficient money already frown at… as if this is a bit 'childish' for them. Whether you are under 18 or Richard Branson reading this, please do the exercise anyway. Sir Richard, if you are reading this, then imagine the days *before* you were super successful. What would you have written down? It's not about status, it's a mind exercise as much as anything else and I implore you to go through the motions whoever you are. In the event of you being extraordinarily wealthy already, maybe what you get out of it is a humbling or joyously appreciative experience that will help you in other ways.

So with mindset to follow I am going to offer you the steps to be hands on with money and of course *what you link with it* rather than money as a commodity itself.

MONEY-HANDS - THE 11 STEPS

STEP 1

The Stock Take

A sombre thought I know, but imagine you were checking out of your current life. Now see this as a move on, achieving a breakthrough into a heavenly realm, joining a religious order if you like. Where you no longer needed any possessions and therefore had to do a huge stock take of everything you owned including the amount of money you have so far accumulated.

STEP 2
Bury The Past

STEP 3
See the Future

STEP 4
Confirm Tools, Contacts & Resources

STEP 5
Create Your Money Blue Print

STEP 6
Think Bigger, Create an Alternative Blue Print

STEP 7
Decide on Your Final Blue Print and Way Forward

STEP 8
Create a Compelling Vision

STEP 9
Decide on New Habits

STEP 10
Monitor, Review, Maintain & Sustain

STEP 11
Get Your Mind Thinking, Attitudes & Beliefs Aligned to Purpose

Character Notes and Steps

WHAT ARE THE MOST IMPORTANT MESSAGES?

ACTION IDEAS

ACTION STEPS – *MY COMMITMENT*

12

Mind-set for Financial Success

All Wealth is Created with the Human Mind
Dale Carnegie

When successful entrepreneurs are asked: "What one thing has made the biggest difference to your success versus others who appear not so fortunate", the overwhelming response is something related to a successful mind-set. This would include things like:

- I never gave up
- I had a powerful vision at all times
- I was inspired by a single all-consuming idea
- It was a challenge I just had to overcome
- The idea driving me created an obsession
- I couldn't stop thinking about it.

What's different about a success mind-set versus a money mind-set? Is there a difference?

In essence these are horses from the same stable, yet there is a big difference. Success can be an achievement that has no money connection. For example, raising money for a charity and getting over a million pounds when you targeted one tenth would give any fund raiser a massive feeling of success. When we look at a money mind-set, this can also be linked to a positive success feeling, however such a feeling only emerges if the money aspect has also worked out.

A business selling pharmaceuticals may be forced to stop making essential life giving drugs to a small number of individuals because it simply isn't making any money, while a business that can afford a loss to look after a similar group of people would feel a sense of achievement and success because they are able to help with money not being a factor.

In writing this book, it's abundantly clear that those who see a money mind-set as key to their goals will probably have not even invested the time and money to read it. Their focus is 'the green stuff' and probably will want all activities to have the acquisition of money at the heart of what they do.

That's why billionaires are still looking for the next opportunity because they have a strong and resolute money mind-set.

The good news is that a success mind-set is simply another option people choose to acquire, and it can of course create a great deal of money. Most well-known musicians were in love with music first. This love created opportunities for success and the money was a bi-product. Very few musicians decide to create new songs in order to make money and the few that do are rarely ever successful because it's more about the money, not the value they bring others.

Even though we all don't want to become a Richard Branson or Deborah Meaden, it is true that without the right mind-set, success becomes less likely. It's also true to observe that those who have a poor money mind-set and also want to be successful fall foul of a number of challenges like the wrong price strategy, choosing the wrong industry or simply forgetting that cash flow and making a profit is part of operating successfully. So let's look at the right mind-set for financial success, and within this 'platform' there is a balance between success and having the right attitude to money.

THE 4 AVENUES FOR FINANCIAL SUCCESS

There is a psychology that you may like to be aware of. Choosing to have the right mind-set sounds a great thing to do, however for most of us the choice has already been made at a very early age in our lives. Based on the psychology of Carl Jung, there are four elements to all of us. There's the direct, focused and 'go for it' type and we all have a greater or lesser element of this inside us.

Let's call this 'Red for Success' thinking. There is also the planner and strategist in our make up too. We can refer to this as 'Blue for Strategy'. Additionally, there's the 'Yellow for Creativity' strand which speaks for itself and finally the 'Green for Partnerships' layer.

Fully appreciating these four catalysts is the first step to getting your financial success mind-set in great shape. By the way, if you are not sure what you are, there are on-line psychological profiling tools available that you can easily find.

So imagine if you are very driven, focused and determined, yet have low creativity. This could mean success with a great deal of hard graft as it were. Equally, someone who is superbly creative can have some of the best ideas in the world, yet doesn't have the drive or strategy to get any of the brainwaves off the ground.

RED FOR SUCCESS

These people have no problem in knowing their purpose and what they wish to achieve. They don't suffer fools gladly, and often have no time for small talk unless it means getting someone on side or as a route to making a sale. They call a spade a spade, and prefer to tell you how it is rather than messing about with being diplomatic. Most of the top brands in the world invariably hire this type of person to run their empire, but The Blue Thinker comes a close second choice. (It's practically unheard of to have a CEO who is a Yellow or Green thinker.

Blue for Strategist

Figures, analysis and planning are the buzz words for this type of individual. They like to think things through, are cautious about making snap decisions - so often they need to reflect and consider things a great deal before they reveal what their plans are. Blue types are comfortable with money and number crunching and often these people end up becoming the financial director of a business.

Yellow for Creativity

"Hey, I've just had a great idea…"

This is a common statement from people in this category. They have lots of good sound ideas. Sometimes their ideas are pinched by others who go off and make lots of money, to the annoyance of these concept creators. The challenge with these guys is that they find it difficult to take an idea and make it into a money spinner or small business. Yet the flip side is that every successful company employs a healthy handful of these type of people in key posts. They are positive, energised, open minded and love to postulate and push the thinking boundaries of other people.

Green for Partnerships

Green people are very aware of other people. In general they seek connections, friendships, business relationships and workable joint ventures and partnerships. The down side is that they are so wrapped up with pleasing and supporting others that they forget to actually make any money. There's no doubt that teamwork, connecting, great communication and aligning people in an organisation to a vision are all very important things, but on its own will not be sufficient to produce tangible trackable results.

The 'Blended Colour' Secret

So it doesn't take much to appreciate what needs to happen around these 4 people zones - avenues to financial success. The bottom line is that you need to be aware of all four areas in your quest to have the right mind-set that would lead you to the success you deserve. You need to have enough 'red' in you to be driven, focused and committed to success. You also need to be a 'blue' strategist who is not shy about figures and spreadsheets. Equally, the 'yellow' in you will give you the zest, passion and creative flair that will differentiate you from the competition. And finally a 'green' streak will allow you to have a motivated, inspired and loyal group of people who you can work with to allow success to be shared rather than all be on your shoulders.

Now you appreciate the bigger picture around mind-set, let's drill down to some important things about your thinking habits, beliefs and paradigms. Let's start by asking you to score yourself. Answer the following 10 questions with a score out of 10. 10 equates to totally agree where 0 is totally disagree and of course any score in between.

FINANCIAL SUCCESS MIND-SET QUIZ

- My parents were very successful financially
- At a very early age I thought about creating money by selling something
- I have always thought about running my very own business
- I am never backward in talking about money when I need to
- I believe I have something valuable to offer others in return for money
- I always negotiate. There's always room for a deal with almost anything
- I love to save money - which I have done from an early age
- I enjoy keeping money but also enjoy spending it wisely
- Unlike time, money is always replaceable
- I have a very positive association between myself and money

Now add up your score. You will have a percentage. Take a look at what it may mean…

0-10

You have a very negative view about money. The chances are this has come about because of your childhood associations. Never despair. Even with such a low score it will be possible to start turning things around. Make sure you read the entire chapter here carefully.

11-20

This low score means you have a poor relationship with money. There is a good chance that your beliefs are based on misunderstandings or incorrect information growing up that you have taken to be true. If you look at the 10 statements above, score out of 10 how much you would love to be able to score each one quite high? Provided this score exceeds 7, you are in good shape to turn things around.

21-30

You probably need to focus on having better faith in yourself. The other question is, is this score about the world at large perhaps not giving you a chance to make it good? Or is it a feeling that you personally are the reason for the apparent lack of money in your life? Either way, acknowledge the number of successful people who were once like you with similar beliefs who managed to do a U turn to a more successful and fulfilling life.

31-40

If you are really serious about being in a better place financially, not all is lost. You may be someone who looks for the lack of opportunity rather than the doors that may lead you to the opportunities. It's like going into a pine forest in autumn looking for pine cones. You will probably see them everywhere. However if you went into the same forest looking for paper cups and came out with a handful - then were asked how many pine cones you saw, you might even say, "I didn't see any!" Time to open your mind to what you want, not thinking about what you lack.

41-50

There isn't a great deal that needs to be done to change your relationship with money. You may even be thinking that you are in the vast majority of people who are 'just average' and in many ways don't expect to be financially well off necessarily. People in this score range will usually have scored a reasonably high score for at least one of the statements. Look again at which one this is for you. Read it a few times. If you scored this one reasonably high, surely it might mean this could be repeated in time for a fair few of the others? You simply need a push in the right direction with a slightly more positive mind-set.

51-60

The good news is that your score is above average. Research shows that if everyone on the planet did this exercise, the vast majority would score themselves below 50. You are therefore in a minority of people who have a better than average association regarding money - which is something to pat yourself on the back for. Hold tight, there is good news heading your way provided you are prepared to follow the ideas in this chapter.

61-70

This is a reasonable score though you are probably wondering, "well if it's reasonable, why don't I have more money in my life?" Two thoughts around the answer to this. If you scored high around saving money, then maybe you are reluctant to take a risk in an entrepreneurial direction? And if you scored high on taking a risk, maybe past risks have not paid off and you are leaning towards caution. The ideal place to be is in the middle. Prepared to take a risk that isn't 'the end of the world' if it failed. And within the pages of this book there will be numerous ways to ensure any small risks you are prepared to take are dramatically minimised. The cautious can and do make money, but sadly are often too old to enjoy it and end up passing it on to their children.

71-80

You are in one of three scoring zones to be proud of. You have a very good relationship with money. If you haven't 'made it' in life yet, you will have a good chance of changing things very swiftly. You will need a bit more self-motivation, self-belief and self-confidence. Yes, it's very much about yourself. You are likely to be someone, with the right inspiration and vision, who can re-write their personal beliefs about money quickly and significantly. This book will tell you how.

81-90

You are in a group of scorers who are already quite successful in life, you have much that others would be envious of, but still feel you need something more to 'pluck the best fruit in the orchard'. Probably the weak area for you is either creativity without the knowledge of what actions need to be taken to transform ideas into monetary benefit, or seed capital and the basics to make an idea come to life, you may simply be lacking the creativity to drive yourself forward with a cracking idea. Either way, the solution is much easier than you could possibly imagine, and lies within these pages.

91-100

Congratulations. You are in the top score zone. And as you were scoring the statements, maybe you were thinking that probably most people would be scoring in a similar way? You are actually in the top 3% of people who have taken this test. The big question is - why are you reading a book like this that you could in fact be writing yourself? There's a chance that what's stopping you is a single belief that needs isolating and then crushing or replacing. If you fail to find out what this is, the danger is going through life being content as opposed to being really happy. The Mind-set Change Card idea would absolutely work for you in a very short time frame, and this idea coming up needs to be followed through without delay!

MONEY = SUCCESS MINDSET

Mindsetter Cards (You get more of what you focus on)

Have you ever wondered how someone becomes a hypochondriac? Not just the odd feeling ill when they're healthy, but the relentless belief building about their bad health that makes them not just feel bad, but even start to display symptoms of their phantom illness. This is a negative example but a powerful one around the power we have in our minds. Equally, we have already explored how we can think ourselves better. (Placebos in a white tablet given to many people and told that they will feel better in 24 hours often do just that. Their symptoms disappear and 'miraculously' they feel well again despite there being nothing but salt in the tablet).

If you think about this mind power logically, what would be easier for the mind to achieve? Making you accept and feel comfortable with money and all the bi-products of acquiring more of it with confidence and ease? Or believing that mind power alone could turn symptoms off and even effect a cure of some of the most deadly diseases that plague humanity?

The really good news is, you don't have to believe in this technique for it to work. Like going to the gym, whether you believe in exercise or not, doing the exercise alone will help you add muscle and feel fitter along with a reasonably healthy diet. So if you are skeptical about something that's going to change your money-success mind-set, that's great! Because it doesn't matter at all. Just do it every day until things start to change - and they will. Then for the sceptic in you, seeing will be believing and you will feel a whole lot better in all sorts of ways…

SETTING UP THE CARDS

Step One: Create a 'Shopping List' of things you most desire. This could range from the perfect home, the ideal car, clothes that would make you feel good, amazing holiday locations, the kind of balances you'd most like to see in your bank accounts and so on. One word of caution is to think about this in terms of ideal not OTT. In other words it would be easy to say you want £100 billion in your current account. However very few people on the planet have this sum to their name and most billionaires will attest to the fact that they are unlikely to ever be able to spend all their money in their lifetime. So think about this in terms of what would make you feel happy and comfortable not delirious and uncomfortable!

Step Two: Create 20-30 statements, each one on a card, each one ideally saying something positive in the present tense. For example:

We love our new 5 bedroom cottage in the heart of the Cotswolds!

My new Mercedes is top of the range and is the best car I have ever owned!

Being financially independent has made such a difference to us all! We are so happy!

Notice it's not about the future, but all about the present. How so? Well if you read a statement every day that says you already have something, your subconscious mind is going to engage and support your desire. If it's about 'I want a 5 bed cottage…' your subconscious is likely to simply think: 'Good luck to you. I look forward to seeing if you get it…'

Once you have your cards ready, read them once a day. Yes, simply read the words on all the cards and then put them away till the next day and repeat the process. When a card becomes reality, save the card somewhere and replace it with a new statement of goal intention. By the way, you may have several cards all about the same goal, simply worded in a different way, or have 20-30 separate goals.

2: GETTING RICH IN 60 MINUTES

Spend 60 minutes writing down how rich you are in non-financial terms. You can do this in linear form or using a mind map, but essentially you should brainstorm everything you can think of that makes you rich in some way. Several years ago a wealthy man blogged that he used to take his children on a holiday to some of the poorest places on the planet. For example he would fly to a poor region of India and stay close to families living on less than $1 a day. Once his kids got back home they started to appreciate the wealth they seemed to be blessed with, and equally appreciated the things that didn't cost a lot of money that many families in the west had, yet rarely appreciated at all. At 16, this is what one of his children wrote after the sixth trip like this.

"Each time we arrived at the destination we'd pick up on something new around not having. This last trip to Ethiopia was tough. I felt embarrassed. Simple things like shoes and a shirt that you get out of the closet and put on were major desires for some of the kids who live here and are simply dying for a hot meal - literally."

You might wonder what this technique is about, and in fact the premise is very straight forward.

Examples to help you spend an hour of your life thinking about what you have as non-financial riches are:

- walking in the rain
- coming home to a hot bath
- eating when you feel like it
- eating for the pleasure of it
- being able to afford transport
- being able to get healthy when you are sick
- a warm bed to sleep in
- friends to be happy around
- education that feeds your mind
- books to read and enjoy
- time to sit quietly and watch the world go past

Of course your personal list would hopefully be more detailed and apply to you in a non-general way. The above list is simply as an example. Now for the final piece to the jigsaw. When you are able to read your list after just 60 minutes, there should be the realisation that you are indeed rich. The chances are - if you could afford to buy this book - you are in the top echelon of the billions of people that live on planet earth, and in that context are rich beyond measure. Once you accept this, it becomes much easier to accept and allow more money into your life because you know what being rich is all about first hand. And whenever you doubt yourself and think rich can only apply to the other guy, re-read your 60-minute list.

3: The Swish Technique

This technique is very effective and exceptionally powerful if done correctly. It originates from NLP (neuro-linguistic programming), and is often used by athletes and top sports people today. Let's explore its use around money-success attraction.

First off we need to create two images. One will be your attitude to a money association that's unhealthy, negative or uncomfortable. Maybe a picture of you looking at other people who have money and success. It could also be someone you know personally, or perhaps are jealous of. The second picture is you in a money-success situation that you would absolutely adore.

Remember not to go too mad in terms of making it outrageously wealthy when such a level of wealth isn't what you ideally want. (What would make you happier - living in a beautiful house with 5-6 bedrooms or a building like Buckingham Palace with 52 royal and guest bedrooms and 188 staff bedrooms?) If it truly is the latter, then fair enough - but do think about what you truly want.

When you have got these two pictures, a bit like still photographs, take the negative one and see it as a huge poster in front of you. Perhaps you will be sitting on a chair and be seeing it straight in front of you. Okay, now look at the edge or border of this big picture and place the positive image as postage stamp size at the base of the poster at the right hand corner. Do look at both pictures in terms of the detail. Be clear on what you are seeing and examine the content as if you will be tested on it.

When you have done this then you are ready for the 'Swish' part. Once again, sit and look ahead at the large poster of the negative picture with the postage stamp size positive image to the bottom right edge of it. The next step is to allow the small image to replace the poster image in a split second - with you making a 'swish' or 'whoosh' sound. The new positive image should have bolder, brighter colours than the negative one to help provide more of an impact.

You should do this several times, and after doing it think about something else which has no connection with the two images.

Do this technique along with reading your cards every day, maybe first thing in the morning and the last thing at night. Persevere with it for at least 30 days, after which you are quite likely to want to keep doing it. Change requires a little commitment which can lead to a great deal of new beliefs that massively and significantly change the quality of your life for the better. When the quality of your life changes, so normally does your financial position for the better.

4: The 'Relative' Think Exercise

Imagine going into a Pound Store. As you browse and shop you know that whatever you pick up is going to be one pound sterling or less. If suddenly an item was marked at £16.99 you would probably want to query it with the manager as it would be completely out of place making you feel very uncomfortable. You certainly are unlikely to want to buy it. Now imagine going into a top quality furniture and bedding store. As you walk around you notice a wooden bed that looks more like a Viking ship priced at £8,854. The duvet on it is marked at £916, and a beautiful small soft silk scatter cushion is marked at £1-50. Are you likely to query this with the manager? Are you feeling uncomfortable with the pricing in a store like this? Are you also not likely to want to buy it because it feels wrong or perhaps that there's something not right with it?

Think about if you were the manager of this store. If someone asked for a discount on the bed, would you knock 30% off? How about just 20%?

Or 10%? It's more likely that you would offer no discount at all, though perhaps do a deal on the delivery charge. The customer in a shop like this is also going to be put off if you start discounting wildly on such a 'quality' item. Many customers have come to this shop because it is reassuringly expensive.

Now think about how much you charge your time out at. We are talking the hourly rate your employer pays you gross. Let's say this amount is £10-30. What would need to happen if you wanted to double that figure? Maybe overtime? Well that's not really doubling the figure, that's working for the same amount by selling more of your time. In any case, overtime is normally easier said than obtainable. The cold reality is you would have to look for a job that would pay you double.

WHAT'S GOING THROUGH YOUR HEAD RIGHT NOW?

- I'd have to leave my industry - £60 an hour for what I do is unheard of
- I don't know anywhere I'd get that kind of money from
- Where would I get such a job from? ...and so on!

Let's imagine you are self-employed and are able to charge more. Currently you charge £80 an hour. Could you see yourself charging £160? What about £240?

- My clients wouldn't buy from me
- I would be too expensive
- Who would be prepared to pay that sort of rate?

But let's stop for a moment and ask where the 'contra questions/statements' come from. They come from our beliefs and what we accept to be true. If we were to create a product/service that offered the value that we wanted in return for the money we sought, what would be the problem?

WOULD THERE EVEN BE A PROBLEM?

The Relative Think Exercise is about thinking bigger in terms of what you desire in return for your time AND what you can offer that would make people still buy from you without hesitation. It applies both to employed, self-employed and entrepreneur. Get this straight in your head and your attitude change will impact your relationship with money and success almost immediately.

5: SUCCESS IMAGING HABIT

One of the most enjoyable and 'luxurious' of all mind-set techniques is this one. Pick some music tracks and a quiet comfortable place to sit. Relax and clear your mind, then start the music. Now create your own mental success video. Allow the most exciting and ideal images to float into the front of your imagination. See yourself and others as part of the montage, and to some extent allow the music to stimulate the thoughts and govern where the mental movie goes next.

Typically you can imagine getting up on a sunny day - from the bedroom of your ideal home, looking out on the garden - getting ready for work, walking around the beautiful house, seeing your family and loved ones, then setting off to... the office? Or your own enterprise? Or is it just another day in paradise?

You'll find with this process that some images will keep re-appearing and that's a good thing. In the event of anything negative coming up, remember you have the power to fix it. In the worst case, change the music track.

If you scored under 50 in the quiz, you should seriously consider doing 2-3 of these exercises and possibly all of them. Aim for a 30 day plan where you simply do not let up until you can feel your attitude towards money and success changing, and of course only stop them completely when you have the life you deserve and the money flow that allows you to enjoy it indefinitely.

Character Notes and Steps

WHAT ARE THE MOST IMPORTANT MESSAGES?

ACTION IDEAS

ACTION STEPS – *MY COMMITMENT*

13

Managing or Imagining?

Money is very much part of all our lives and something we can rarely opt out of. As a result we have to see it in the same context as food, water and shelter. It's a given that is inextricably part of the fabric of life itself, yet astonishingly, only recently has it been something being taught in schools. We have a curious educational system that expects students to study, memorise and pass exams yet invariably offers to help our insights in these essential skills. It's like giving someone a parachute, strapping it on their back and then pushing them out of a place devoid of all instructions. And so it is with money.

One of the biggest and most significant pieces of advice that could ever be given to anyone no matter how old they are is *to save*. Yet we are put off by the feeling that it may be a chore to do this, would be of little value because they probably *couldn't afford it* and so on. In the realm of offering professional financial services, the topic least discussed is short term saving. This too is somewhat unbelievable given that there is no rocket science behind it. Recently, in doing a personal financial review, an independent financial adviser spotted a banker's order in place for £96.18. On closer inspection it was for some sort of household insurance package and this payment had gone out for the past 8 years and 11 months. This equates to a staggering £10,291.26. The main problem with it however is that the family were already insured by their mortgage company so this non-refundable payment was superfluous and no longer needed.

Curiously this same family had also said that they were unable to save anything because they had no opportunity to do so!

There is a world of difference between money managing and *money imagining*. One is operational where the second is being money proactive. We review brochures for our holidays, window shop in show rooms for new pieces of furniture and sometimes over spend on Christmas and birthdays, yet most of us seem to want to run a mile when it comes down to doing something exciting with the money that passes through our fingers each month. Given that we tend to get what we focus on, the first step to making a difference with your finances is to spend a good half a day looking at *money past, money present and money future*.

MONEY PAST

There's a good reason for keeping old statements and money related paperwork, because it creates a trail we can look back on. For example if you have several credit cards and never pay them off in full at the end of the month, it's an interesting exercise to work out how much interest you have paid on each card over the past 5-10 years. But I warn you that you may also need a stiff drink on stand by! Equally working out what you've paid for utilities, holidays, food, fuel, house and car repairs, communication, internet/media all tell self contained stories in their own right. Knowing the past will help you deal with the present and future so much better, though the downside is the potentially numbing feeling of regret and wishing you hadn't used 'ostrich' financial planning by being blissfully unaware of your past situation and related financial decisions.

MONEY PRESENT

Do also read the chapter on the 'Money Map'. In my experience, few people ever have a grounded and clear picture of their finances. For many, their finances would be described as being sporadic or haphazard or plain simply a mess. They often have little shape, thought through plans or exciting money horizon to look towards each month.

You can start with an outgoings list. Put down everything that's already on a standing order or direct debit. Then a separate list for known expenses in the year that you probably do not budget for like car repairs, clothes, household emergencies and the 'unexpected'. Do remember trips out to the cinema, theatre and eating out under an entertainment section too!

Creating a plan that takes into account all these things might seem unnecessary, yet having something in place is better than being faced with things that simply were not accounted for. That's why a money map works well here. You can actually map out all your finances and truly know where urgent changes need to be made. Those who go through the possible discomfort of mapping out their finances verses living in nothing more than a financial quagmire find the so-called pain worth every penny.

MONEY FUTURE

Having pencilled out the past and present with all the supporting paperwork - almost as if you are preparing for the annual accounts for a business, you will be allowed to consider the more stimulating aspect - the financial future.

So far you may have not set up the savings aspects, but even if you already save as a habit, how excited do you feel about what you are saving? And are your savings in accounts with nothing more than an account number, or do you have savings accounts with names?

Like Holiday Account, Clothes Account, Entertainment Account, General Spending Account, Emergency Account and so on… Provided you stick with only spending from the designated account, you will take a few months to get into the swing, but after this you will begin to smile at the simplistic ingenuity of such imagining versus the old fashioned boring *managing.*

What follows is a methodology to switch from money managing to money imagining. Go through these steps and record the answers to the questions. If nothing else the results could be more than just revealing, they could be both deeply insightful and/or inspiring!

MY MONEY

<u>REGULAR MONTHLY AMOUNT COMING IN</u>

£

LESS - HARD OUTGOINGS (THESE HAVE TO BE PAID)

Gas	Council Tax
Electric	Car Tax
Water	Car Insurance
Other Utilities	Other Car-related Payments
TV Licence/Media/Wi-fi	Mortgage/s
Mobile Phone	Monthly Food
Landline Phone	Travel/Commuting Costs
Insurances	Credit Cards (stipulate)
Regular savings	Loans(stipulate)
Subscriptions/memberships (stipulate)	Other Regular Payments (stipulate)

TOTAL   £   .

This amount you absolutely need to find each month.

LESS - SOFT OUTGOINGS

These could be cancelled easily in an emergency. List them. Some may be moved from the previous list if you decide they can become flexible. So whilst you still need to find the amount each month, remember that they need to be able to be changed/ removed if needed.

TOTAL   £   .

FINAL DISPOSABLE INCOME TOTAL   £   .

This amount is the minimum you need to save from TODAY. Create a separate account for this where there are NO withdrawals. Add additional ad hoc sums whenever you can.

In order to help you structure this into a format that you can genuinely use I've included a formal Income v Expenditure form that my financial planning business has used over many years successfully. For some of you it may well be the first time that you see what happens with your money each month.

£ Income & Expenditure £

MONTHLY OUTGOINGS

MONTHLY INCOME

Payment to Lender

Life Assurance

Buildings Insurance

Contents Insurance

Gas

Electricity

Telephone

Water Rates

Property Tax

Hire Purchase

Credit Cards

Other Loans (specify)

Pension

Food

Clothing

Entertainment

Vehicle Tax

Vehicle Insurance

Petrol

Servicing / Repairs

TV & Video Rental

Miscellaneous

Salary / Wages

Investment Income

Other Income

Total Amounts

Total Outgoings:

Total Income:

Net Income (+/ -)

Comments / Observations / Recommendations:

Character Notes and Steps

WHAT ARE THE MOST IMPORTANT MESSAGES?

ACTION IDEAS

ACTION STEPS – *MY COMMITMENT*

14

DO NOT READ THIS CHAPTER!

Last Ditch Routes to More Money & Greater Wealth

Warning:

This Chapter is for people who have read all the other chapters but feel they are still no further forward in knowing how to improve their finances, personal wealth and well being. It's a last ditch read for those of you who really feel their back is against the wall.

If after reading this there is still no light at the end of the tunnel, then perhaps there is nowhere else to turn - which is why you should AVOID reading it...

Only read on if you feel you absolutely need more help. For some this is the 'Trouble Shooting Chapter' for others it's the 'Belt and Braces' Options. But if you are able to avoid it, you will always know that you may come back to it if you absolutely have to... It's the ace up your sleeve.

TOP BARRIERS TO WEALTH

MONEY PHOBIA?

There are more people with this ailment than you can imagine. The phobia can take different 'shapes'. There are those who hate numbers and simply have a form of number blindness around figures. Others have neuro-associated links to money and finances and rather not be involved with it, other than spending it, which very few people with money phobia are not able to carry out. Let's expand now more specifically how the phobia can manifest in people.

Why don't you consider a set of sessions with either a personal coach or a hypnotherapist? The latter would be the final solution, but this kind of person who is experienced could make a big difference.

I Am Too Young

We covered this at the start. Why does this still trouble you?

And…what a great problem to have! You are at the start of a financial journey with the seeds of a 'Money Tree' in your hands. The fact that you have no significant money yet is perhaps overshadowed by something you are missing… time. Time is the one main thing that is far more valuable than mere money. The more you have of it, the better. Where you can always obtain more money, you will never be able to beg, steal, borrow or acquire more time in your personal 'time bank account'.

Remember from before. If you were aged 20 and to simply save as much as you could every month in excess of 10%, then invest the money into a relatively safe investment, by age 50 you could be a millionaire. You would be quite well off financially by default. However this is a very safe strategy. There are many other avenues you can take that will still take you quite far in your quest to amass wealth. You will also be aware that financial institutions and venture capitalists like youth and are more prepared sometimes to help those starting out. Youth definitely has its advantages. If you are young you are already wealthy in an indirect way.

So if you are young, first look at all the friends and contacts of your age around you. How many of them would you go into business with? The chances very few. How many of them would have read this book? Probably even less. This makes you different. Now imagine getting into a small business or money stream. Then compare yourself with those same people. Would you agree that they are probably in exactly the same financial positions with the same money mentality but just a year on? This could be your opportunity of a lifetime. Personally I believe in coincidence less and less these days. When something happens my gut feel is that Life, Nature, God or something greater than you is helping you. See the open door for what it is, and push on it hard and fast because most people around you are not seeing the door as you do…

I Am Too Old

We covered this too. Being older has advantages. The first one is experience and knowledge. Someone who is old is also looking for much less success than people with a lot of time on their side. At 20 you would £2-3m to be free financially for life, but at 65 this sum could be as little as £250,000. Your target can be much smaller and highly achievable faster as a result.

If you're 'old' you are likely to be more focused on what you want, have a better understanding of what it is you're seeking and less likely to mess around in the attainment of your financial goals.

There are a whole string of people who started out late and finished in time to enjoy the spoils of their labours. These people didn't just do it by saving money but using it wisely in short-term opportunities. Many were of course business-related. If you're older and seek more money, the chances are your financial planning to date has been less than successful. This means that ideally you are looking for a stream of money to supplement your income where you are not having to work. Have you thought of investigating as to how others have achieved this at your age? They are out there, and if you have not researched it why would you not want to do that as a next step?

If you own your own home you may want to consider using some of the capital wisely. If you are thinking of keeping the home to pass on then why not go into a business with say your children who are to benefit from this inheritance because with a business that gives you income, it will boost their inheritance at the same time. And it can be inheritance tax efficient!

I Have No Capital

The majority of people in the world are short of capital. For whatever reason, they do not have the funds to supplement their thinking, dreams and desires. However, this by and large does not stand in the way of someone determined to turn their financial position around. Capital may be obtained from loans or the sale of shares. Occasionally grants can help provide you with starting capital depending on the type of business. What produces such capital is the idea you have in the first place. If it is well presented, capital is never a problem to anyone. Indeed, people will be chasing you with cheque-book in hand. So forget the capital, think about the idea. And coming up with an idea isn't necessarily about originality, given that apparently there are no new ideas any more.

Consider this. If you came up with a good idea, researched it, got some financials around it and did everything bar starting up a business around it, do you not think it would be possible to sell your package for a sum of money? You could trademark or patent the idea if it's a good one and then it would really have some value. Equally, sell 80% for cash and keep a 20% income on dividend pay out thereafter. I am not suggesting this is easy, but until you get up and decide to do something about it, you will always be in the position you are in now…wondering.

I Dislike Money, Hate Having To Find It, Yet Need It

This is a tricky one, yet more common than you may suppose. There are many people who are not motivated by money itself yet appreciate they need it in order to have the lifestyle that does motivate and inspire them.

One such person may be singer Elton John. There have been many articles about how he loves spending large amounts of money on fresh flowers as one of his daily spends and apparently the bill can run into hundreds of thousands of pounds a year, so it has been reported. With other reports on his money mindset he comes across as a generous fun loving person who spends a great deal and has had to hit the brakes on spending when more was going out than coming in.

His means of making money apart from appearances is largely through music royalties. I have never met him so I don't know how he would have felt if he had taken a different path in life and got a regular office job. I suspect he may have been in the 'hate having to acquire money but adore spending or giving it away to deserving causes'. What keeps him solvent is being lucky/good enough to make money in a way he absolutely adores in a profession that, at his level, pays him exceptionally large sums compared with most people.

In having a dislike for money, think about your liking for financial freedom, so when you think money you are associating freedom with it. Then decide to face what you dislike and deal with it rather than constantly appear to run away from it. Go back in this book and re-read it with the express intention of finding two or three things that you are prepared to do - then do it and maybe even start to enjoy it. When I was at school, on a Thursday night I would often do all my homework for Monday morning, though being aware that most of my school mates would leave it until Sunday evening (or not do it at all!). There is something cathartic about doing what you least want to do, but know you *need to do* and simply get it done.

Frequent action taken in any set direction will always build in terms of outcome and a desire to keep doing it. Physical exercise is one such thing. You may start off hating the idea, then you make yourself, then you start to see benefits, so you do some more, see more benefits, do much more, start to enjoy it, then wonder why you ever thought negative thoughts about it.

I Have No Motivation To Make More Money (But Want It)

Motivation comes from movement. This is most certainly true in a sports situation and also refers to the mental movement of ideas and the responses to things that may start to go in your favour.

In order for motivation to exist, you need to be involved in a small level activity that creates results.

Thought + Action = Result

In effect to start with it doesn't matter what the result is. However, no thought will lead to no action and therefore no result. It's a bit like people who work in a sales situation with a telephone. If they make 100 calls totally blind, statistically three people will show interest and one person is likely to buy from them.

Knowing this, the motivation comes from calling the 100 people as quickly as possible in order to get to that one sale based on pure statistics. This then becomes their motivation.

Unless you are doing something regularly towards more money in your life, to some extent not worried about what the actions are, yet ensuring that action is being taken in the right direction regularly, this alone will start results beginning to emerge which will lead to a small number of positive outcomes. Statistics alone tell you this. More motivation will come from improving the process and getting better results.

There are many other ways of motivating yourself and there are a number of self-development books out there that are inspiring and supportive. Classic ones: *The Magic of Thinking Big* and *Think & Grow Rich*. Read these and re-check your motivation level. Then watch *The Secret DVD*. I think you will then be feeling very different. If you would like a free mindset audio to help, e-mail me: *results@deanthorpe.com*

I Have Low Self-Esteem

Low self-esteem is something that can be fixed relatively quickly. The first step is wanting to fix it and acknowledging that it is one of those challenges that is highly fixable.

Something you can do to improve this - ask for positive feedback from as many people who know you. This part is important as it's not general feedback it is **positive** feedback. In other words what do they like about you, who you are, what you do, how you do it and so. It's often surprising when you realise that you yourself often overlook the good things about you and also rarely ask others for their opinion.

A useful exercise is to shut yourself in a safe place to relax and think about your low self-esteem being a literal barrier to success perhaps in the form of brick wall? Then imagine a large amount of cash trying to break through to you, however being held back by the brick wall. Although this is a visualisation it's pointing to reality. A few simple negative thoughts in your mind is holding money at bay because you are putting your beliefs around what you think of yourself in the way of the success you rightly deserve. Repeat this visualisation exercise every day for the next 30 days and notice how your self esteem improves considerably.

I Am Not Creative

It's easy to counter this thought with - of course you are creative and highly imaginative - yet this in itself is unlikely to sway your core belief. And it is a belief that you have selected, probably at a very early stage of your life. What's worse is that the belief has been installed in your belief system by external factors, which may include someone close to you like a parent, sibling, teacher or friend. If you imagine just for a moment that being the creative you could unleash ideas that may be transformed into large volumes of cash, you will readily appreciate how amazing life could be if you could eliminate your limiting belief.

A starting point would be to think about the many ideas that are not creative, yet still make money for those who came up with them. Look at some of the road signs and the relatively simple art work involved, knowing that the artists probably made a large sum of money for these now well-known images. There are also many so-called creative people who also believed they were not creative - yet do you believe they are able to think about what they need to produce, are prepared to do the work involved and will have another go if their first attempt fails? We see them as creative yet they see themselves as hard workers. Do what they do and potentially you become creative in the same way. Surely it's not about being creative here - it's about coming up with concepts and ideas that you can sell and become wealthy from.

I have Poor Money Retention Habits

Throughout this book there are many ideas for habits around creating and keeping more money to yourself. If you believe your current habits are letting you down, then you need to create new ones as soon as possible. For the habit to become something you don't have to think about, you will need to force yourself to keep the habit for at least 30 days. After this your belief about having poor money retention habits will begin to fade.

Other great habits include:

- *having separate accounts in how you deal with money. For example, holiday account, a fun account, an education account, a savings account and even spending account.*

- *always carrying a chunk of money with you wherever you go. Say, £50. Never to be spent yet to give you a feeling that you're not short of cash at any point in time.*

- *having the urge to identify a small amount of cash that you can set aside and save in an account where you never ever check the balance.*

I Hate Risking My Money

Being risk averse is normally a good thing about money. At the same time you do need to consider ways for those of us who want considerably more than a bank interest rate, especially when interest rates are artificially low and likely to remain so. A way to reduce risk and yet not lose everything is to take a more measured approach by investing the money or funds across pooled investments and different types of assets. You can set up a separate account and save your 'risk money' separately and think about it as cash you can afford to lose in your pursuit of increasing your wealth. This does not mean that you actually go out to waste money but that there is no anguish if the worst happens and you do lose it.

Cash is always king and having some set aside gives you the power to consider more options carefully - and go places that other people without cash fear to tread. There's also a big difference between a reasonable risk and a foolhardy one. In risking cash you alleviate the possibility of losses by having some control over it. The biggest way to risk and lose money has to be parting with your cash and giving a third-party full reign over it. Dislike in risking money this way is very healthy indeed.

I Know Nothing About Starting A Business

You may be aware that people like Richard Branson fell into the business world rather than set out to create his global business empire. He candidly explains that terminology like *cash flow forecast* is something he got to understand after many years of successful trading. This does indicate that to be successful in business you don't have to be a business success in the first place - nor have special training or knowledge. Now although this would be helpful of course, there will always be ways to get around this.

SOLUTIONS TO WEALTH CREATION

When Time is the Solution in Chunks

Time is a great solution to procuring wealth as already discussed previously, it's possible to pinch little chunks of time throughout a period of a week for example - particularly if you have a full-time occupation elsewhere. Time then, set aside for a money making project can be a great asset if managed advantageously.

When Timing is the Solution

Timing is a major solution to greater wealth as any top marketing consultant will attest to. Knowing what's popular and capitalising upon it at the right time has made many people wealthy overnight. The downside is leaving it too late to enter the market place. For example, companies are still attempting to enter the coffee outlet opportunity alongside the major players who got there first. Unless these 'newbies' can come up with something truly fresh and original, and have the where with all to build a business around it, they are likely to be throwing away their investment capital. In summary here, if you have the time and an idea whose time has come, you are streets ahead in starting a potentially successful venture. To find out consider doing a survey with 100 people you know. This information could be dynamite.

When Lack of Help is a Solution

With the help of the internet, you are never alone when help is needed. It's common to feel isolated and unable to act on your own if there's no-one to help you into a money production venture. Yet you will probably find all you need by looking on-line. You can practically outsource every aspect of a business today. It can also be beneficial to deal with comparative strangers in a business-like way where you can better negotiate terms to your advantage.

When People Around Me Is A Solution

Like-minded souls in a venture together can be powerful and motivational, though be careful too because partnerships in business can be very fragile. The best time this kind of arrangement works is when everyone in the group has a completely different role and each individual is contributing to the collective without too much 'overlap' in roles going on. So what are the people components of a business you might decide to set up?

The Overall Leader. Someone who is focused on outcomes and results and can be quite dispassionate about how these are strategically achieved, finding it easy to make decisions in a logical rather than emotional way.

The Organiser. This person's strength is of an operational nature and is good at knowing how to keep tabs on what's going on, where everything is, and how to be organised going forward.

The Technologist. A wizard with anything technical. Can specify what technology is needed and how to get the best/most from this aspect.

The Sales & Marketing Guru. As the title suggests, a person who is at home with sales, selling, communicating business messages and acquiring new opportunities.

The Creative. The individual who can see things in a different light rather than a traditional one.

The Dependable. You may need more than one of these. People who are happy to simply get on with the job in hand and loyal with it. Can be a tall order, but such people do exist.

When a Business Start-Up is the Solution

The 12-Point Business Start Up (Primary Items) Checklist

Why?

Why am I starting a business? Is this the only way to go? Have I researched, asked professional people the right questions? Made a decision based on looking at all the options, facts and advice available?

What?

What is the business about? What does it do? How would I describe it in a few words? Does it have a good name? Have I thought about its brand? Does it excite me?

How?

How will it operate? How will I start it?

Who?

Who will be in it apart from myself? Who would be the first type of person I should look for to join me? (What will their role be?)

What if?

What if it doesn't work to begin with? (What are my contingency plans?) What if it's super successful - can I cope with this outcome?

Where?

Where will it be based? Can I operate from home to start and save overheads? Does it need an office from day one?

Entity?

Do I set it up as a limited company? What are the implications of this versus not going this route?

Business Plan?

Who will create the business plan? If it's me, do I know how to write one? Where can I get a sample one from to check out?

Advisors?

What advisors should I have in place from the start. For example - business banker, accountant, business coach, legal adviser, financial adviser.

Technology?

Who will look after this aspect? Should I choose IOS, Linux or Windows?

Capital?

Do I have any to invest? If I need some, where would I go first? How can I convince others to invest if this is the route I take?

When?

When do I start the business?

WHEN I AM THE SOLUTION

The ultimate consideration as a solution to wealth creation is - yourself. Everything in this book hinges on you in reality. With the best ideas ever, nothing will transpire unless you are convinced you can do it, and have every intention of giving it your best shot.

The truth is, if you have the right beliefs in yourself, your attitude, behaviour and results will fall into place regardless. Belief in yourself is everything.

Go to any place where they have an escalator and notice how the majority of people want to stand on it and allow the machinery to do all the work. This is a typical scenario at a busy railway station or airport. The user will plonk themselves on the travelling staircase and make little effort to do anything themselves. This also applies to young nimble and agile escalator users. Sadly, the vast majority of humans are not prepared to make an effort. They fail to value time and are looking for the easy option. However, a much smaller group will climb the escalator if they can get past the 'standers'. They want to get to the summit and get on with other things rather than waste time standing still. Perhaps these individuals are the true entrepreneurs where the 'standers' are those who want things given to them. And we know that the acquisition of more money is not something that is normally given to people without something in return being required.

<u>THE ESCALATOR</u>

There was an experiment at a station where an escalator was next to a set of stone stairs.

On day 1, passengers were filmed choosing the escalator in preference to climbing the stairs. At the end of the day, the stone stairs were transformed into a working piano keyboard - and passengers were filmed on day 2. And what a massive difference on the second day! The majority were now going up the stairs and not using the escalator because it was much more fun.

The learning here is that we as humans can be tempted to take action if the action has a fun or enjoyable element attached. It's worth thinking about this because if the money solution you create has no fun or enjoyment it's not likely to succeed for you.

If you start your own fruit juice bar, then you need to love fruit, enjoy getting others to drink it, and thoroughly love the idea of serving it and charging for your great range of health-giving products.

Staying with Escalators, there is a great clip YouTube called *Stuck on an Escalator - Take Action*. It's a funny yet poignant look at two people 'stuck' on a broken down escalator and watching them react as if they are stuck in a lift.

So often we apply this insane thinking to barriers to our success. We get stuck but apply it to previous occasions without fully investigating why we are truly stuck... and whether there is a solution staring at us in the face. Of course, in this amusing clip, these people can easily just walk off to freedom, instead they prefer to stay put on a defective escalator - waiting to be rescued!

One of my favourite stories about mindset is that of a general of the Persian Army two hundred years ago. A spy was caught and brought before him. It was usual in these cases for the spy to be shot by a firing squad, but the man of some compassion tended to give captured spies a choice. They could be shot against a wall or walk through the Bronze Door. On this occasion he asked the spy what he would prefer. When the spy asked what was behind the door, the general said he had to discover this for himself.

After a brief moment of deliberation, the spy chose the firing squad, and the execution was carried out. Afterwards an aide of the general asked his superior, "What lies behind the Bronze Door sir?"

"Freedom, and I have only ever known one man to take it..."

You do have a choice. The known way, which currently doesn't work for you or going through a door that may lead to the financial freedom you would love to achieve…

EPILOGUE

If you are still reading this chapter and realise you have come to the end with a feeling of not being inspired, dismiss this book and all its concepts and resign yourself to the fact that there is no real way you can increase the money in your life. You must put up with what you have or even consider appreciating it and being satisfied with your lot?

Alternatively, go back in the book, read it again and note everything you need to do to turn your financial ship around. Then *take action*. Especially the action that doesn't require a penny of investment.

Wishing you Every Success
Dean Thorpe